As the new millenium unfolds, countless stories of alien abductions have begun to penetrate the mainstream consciousness of mankind. While some new insights into the human condition have been obtained, too few of these accounts have brought such experiences to a level where they can be consumed and digested into a profitable understanding for the individual reader.

Montauk: The Alien Connection unravels the remarkable story of Stewart Swerdlow, a gifted mentalist who has experienced extrasensory perception since birth. Stewart's rare abilities not only made him a magnet for government surveillance, but his unique genetic structure made him a clearing house for different alien agendas which sought him out for their own purposes. Everyone's sinister plans went haywire after Stewart began a deprogramming procedure with Preston Nichols which was designed to clear his memories and the controlling influences which had been installed. Stewart was subsequently threatened and eventually jailed after refusing to comply with orders to sever his ties with Nichols. Despite this, the full truth began to work its way into his life.

Estranged from his family, Stewart was sent to prison as a financially destitute and hopeless, tragic figure. Despite a severe human struggle, he was able to call on his own God-given abilities, reshuffle the deck, and reevaluate his life and the various agencies and entities which sought to utilize him. Weeding out the negative influences, Stewart was able to recover key memories and discard those forces which sought to entrap him as well as mankind. The most intriguing aspect of his incredible story is that he has a valuable legacy to share.

D1453608

Cover Art: *The Original Butterfly*

---

*Artist's conception
of the prototype for the original
butterfly who donated DNA for Project Earth
in order to create the creatures on Earth known as
butterflies. The glyph inlaid on the upper right of the
archway is an archetypal symbol signifying the opening
up of DNA. The glyph on the upper left of the archway
represents the perfection of physical realities. In this
rendition, the butterfly has mixed its DNA with a
human creature. Butterflies on Earth monitor
magnetism and know how to adjust it so
that it has a beneficial effect on
the environment.*

MONTAUK

THE ALIEN CONNECTION

STEWART SWERDLOW
EDITED BY PETER MOON

ILLUSTRATED BY NINA ANUE

Sky Books

NEW YORK

Montauk: The Alien Connection
Copyright © 1998 by Expansions Publishing Company
First printing, January 1998

Cover illustration by Nina Anue
Typography and book design by Creative Circle Inc.
Editor: Peter Moon, assisted by Janet Swerdlow
Published by: Sky Books
      Box 769
      Westbury, New York 11590

DISCLAIMER Nothing in this book should be interpreted to be an attack on
the United States Government or its duly appointed legal representatives. The
publisher and the author believe and fully support the United States Government as set forth by the U.S. Constitution. It is further noted that as this book
may be considered controversial to some people, the publisher and author wish
to state their belief that all people are created with equal human rights and that
all nations, races and religions derive from a common source that embraces the
brotherhood of all creatures. No offenses or possible inadvertent slights are
intended toward any race, religion or ethnicity.

Library of Congress Cataloging-in-Publication Data
_____

Stewart Swerdlow
    Montauk: The Alien Connection
    252 pages
    ISBN 0-9631889-8-4
1. Aliens 2. UFOs 3. Montauk
Library of Congress Catalog Card Number 97-062051

This book is dedicated to Janet Swerdlow
for her devotion, tenacity, caring, and unconditional love.
And, to all of my children, who gave me strength
and hope to go on during my darkest hours.

CONTENTS

INTRODUCTION

As I write this introduction, humanity is undergoing a radical change in the way it views space and time. Once thought to be the exclusive realm of learned physicists and mathematicians, we have learned that our "sacred" institutions and universities have lied about space and time. If we are to be more gracious, we will say that they have simply misstated the facts.

Fortunately or unfortunately, the secrets of space and time have not been handed to us on a silver platter. Instead, they have been given to us piecemeal as if a stage magician's apprentice was leaking out his master's trade secrets. The magician does not want to give up his act! Thus, we are forced to cope with whatever information comes our way rather than attend a "University of Space-Time Consciousness."

The biggest secret of time and space that has been unlocked is that these very components of our physicality can be manipulated. This is still a novel idea to conventional scientists, scholars, and news media who are manipulated from birth. Manipulation of consciousness comes under the heading of "mind control," a subject which has never been fully embraced by major media.

Unfortunately, when we embrace the consciousness aspects of space-time, we are dealing with mind control. The reason for this is that our responses to the very idea of space-time are, by and large, conditioned responses. There are few who ever seriously and successfully question the structure of physical reality as we know it. While the evolution of nature and the human brain might at first glance seem to be the innocent culprit in this equation, it is not that simple. The human brain is actually a perfect computer which is fully capable of serving as a tool for cosmic enlightenment to its host. The problem is that this response in mankind has been short-circuited due to any number of various factors. These could include aliens, ancient priesthoods, religious indoctrination, youth groups, and the CIA's documented mind control program known as MK-Ultra.

MK-Ultra was a 20th century "modernization" of ancient techniques such as those employed by the ancient *Assassins*, a Middle Eastern cult during the Middle Ages who programmed subjects to kill through the use of hashish. After World War II, the government began to experiment with narcosynthesis or "truth serum" drugs. This has been documented and is not really denied by the government, however its full significance has been minimized in the extreme sense of the word. Books on such topics usually focus on the treatment of prisoners of war and tend to confine the subject to wresting wartime secrets from the enemy. Sometimes, a more bold approach will investigate the assassination potentials of mind control and the concept of turning human beings into programmed robots. This is a step in the right direction as far as discovering the truth, but it does not go far enough.

If you can accept the simple premise that unscrupulous people have worked within the sphere of the government's truth serum project, a far more amazing scenario presents itself. When a human being is put under the procedure of narcosynthesis, his subconscious can be accessed without him even being aware of what is said. Under most conditions, he will tell the truth. What is even more remarkable is that he can tell the truth about things he does not even know in his conscious mind. The subject can be used to tap the collective unconscious.

Of course, any curious and diligent researcher will go far beyond the prospect of asking only for wartime secrets. He will ask about God, the history of evolution, and the very nature of reality. He will not pull any punches. Of course, some narcosynthesis subjects are more attuned than others to this sort of research and many clinical studies would be done. Through the human psyche, research could be pursued that would be unprecedented in terms of human understanding. If you put someone like Einstein under the serum, you might begin to get some pretty interesting insights concerning the dilemma of the universe. At some point, some researcher is going to do his best to tap the principles of creation that remain hidden to our perceptions of "everyday normal reality." When one penetrates these hidden control zones of consciousness, one embraces what is commonly known as the "occult."

What I have said above is a simple premise that anyone can accept with common logic. The actual history of such research is another matter, and although some of it is documented, the juiciest parts tend to remain somewhat hidden. We do know that wild experimentation with LSD was indulged in the 1950's as well as tortuous mind control under the tutelage of Dr. Ewen Cameron. Much of the LSD research was done under the tutelage of Dr. Timothy Leary, a Harvard professor who became a public mockery in the 1960's. Although Leary claimed he was using the CIA to fund his research, the intelligence community was also using him. Whatever the truth was about Leary, he was just one leg of what is known as the Monarch Project, a mind control research endeavor that was predominant in the 1950's. Leary and his brethren were sometimes known as the "Monarch Boys." The latter day evolution of this mind control research was centered at the Camp Hero facility at Montauk Point, New York.

Much of what we know about the research at Montauk has been supplied by Preston Nichols, a man who was part of this mind control research both as practitioner and victim. He has coauthored various books on the subject with myself. A synopsis of this work has been included in the appendix for those who are not already familiar with it. In past books, Preston has had much to say about "Montauk boys," a colloquial term that refers to anyone who has been mentally programmed through their sexual psyche. He has also recently applied this term to women which he now refers to as "Montauk girls."

What is perhaps most disturbing about Preston's research is that there is no shortage of such programmed people. They exist in the hundreds across Long Island and that is probably just a small sampling. There are numerous people who could testify that they have been part of strange mind control experiments. They usually have fragmented memories that indulge the very bizarre. The lives of these people are often a testimony that weirdness, usually in the form of manipulative mind control techniques, has been perpetrated upon them.

This brings us to our present topic and the subject of this book: an individual who has suffered through such experiments and lived to tell his story. His name is Stewart Swerdlow.

I first heard of Stewart Swerdlow in 1992 when I was still finishing up the manuscript for *The Montauk Project: Experiments in Time*. Preston was telling me wild stories about Stewart's deprogramming procedure. The stories were so incredible that I personally wondered whether or not Stewart even existed.

Later, I saw a video-taped testimony of Stewart Swerdlow and his involvement in mind control experiments, some of which included the Montauk Project. I knew the character was real now.

The next event I learned concerning Stewart was that he was going to prison under the most bizarre circumstances. After beginning to work with Preston Nichols in an effort to recover his memories, the government began to prosecute him for crimes of which he had no proper memory. As a corporate controller, his name was forged on checks which had been issued *with* the full knowledge of his employers. The charge was embezzlement, but the real crime was entrapment (of him).

After these charges were made against Stewart, I soon heard that Geraldo Rivera was going to do a show on UFO abductions with Stewart as the main point of interest. At the last minute, Stewart pulled out of the show because he was being threatened with more jail time if he went on the air. Even though he did not appear on television, Stewart was given a harsh sentence. The judge was sympathetic and seemed to believe that Stewart had limited culpability, if any, but he claimed to have no choice but to follow the softest of the sentencing guidelines. This meant three years in prison.

After Stewart began serving his sentence, I started writing *Montauk Revisited*. The purpose of the book was to attempt to corroborate that the Montauk Project did, in fact, exist. There were various degrees of proof and various trails to pursue. Stewart's involvement became most evident when I received a phone call from a woman I call Elaine Donald. Stewart refers to her in this book as a woman with a Brooklyn accent. Elaine requested I come to her apartment and discuss Stewart with her. Nothing should be said over the phone. Upon telling Preston of our conversation, he said Elaine was an "FBI backed psychic." This means that she did psychic readings by first telling the person she would get back to them. She then checked them out independently. After that, she consulted their FBI file through a contact at the agency. Of course, such a file does not refer to ordinary criminal files. These are a hidden tier of files the government presumably has on all of us. It might not be the FBI but really the CIA. I don't know if Preston was right, but she does her psychic readings after first investigating the client and getting back to them later.

Elaine was adamant about Stewart having nothing to do with Montauk and that everything attributed to his involvement originated from Preston. She portrayed herself as Stewart's friend. I thought it absurd that she had me come all the way to her house and expect me to believe her just on her word. I was still skeptical about Stewart myself, but her words convinced me something odd was afoot. It became more absurd when she called up a friend of hers in Massachusetts. This is a woman I call Mary Snodgrass. She also tried to convince me that Stewart was not involved at Montauk. This woman's comments were even more absurd. When I was informed that Stewart had disavowed all connection to the Montauk Project since being in jail, I offered a counter-theory. I informed her that there is no way to ensure he wasn't gotten to in prison and programmed. She assured me this was not the case and, as proof, said that the prison guards had assured her of this. A statement like this is like getting the fox to swear that the chicken coop is locked up and well protected. What was more absurd was that she actually expected me to believe this. She must have thought that my ability to discern facts was nonexistent. Preston later informed me that Mary Snodgrass was part of the CIA affiliated Aquarius Group.

When Mary read my account of her in *Montauk Revisited*, she was upset, but it represented her quite accurately.

I discussed all of this with Preston and whether we should use the above in the book. We both decided it would be best to write to Stewart and ask him. After a few weeks, I received a typed reply from Stewart in which he denounced Preston and the Montauk Project. At first glance, this seemed like a negative response to me. What I did not know at the time was that, before he went to prison, Stewart vowed that he was on Preston's side in uncovering the Montauk Project and would not recant. If he were forced to toe the line in prison, he would go with the flow. If he wrote anything typed to Preston, that information would be considered tainted and written under the influence of his masters. If he wrote a letter by hand, it would signify that those words were his real intention.

As the letter I received from Stewart was addressed to me and not Preston, this put some doubt on the matter. Accordingly, Preston decided we should use a fictitious name to describe Stewart. I chose the name Stan Campbell and that is how he is described in *Montauk Revisited*.

I did not meet Stewart until August 12, 1996. We took a trip out to Montauk Point. Almost immediately, he asked my opinion of Elaine Donald. When I gave him a negative opinion, he told me that he did not trust her and that she had not acted in his best interests. He further disavowed Mary Snodgrass, said she manipulated people, and had also dictated verbatim the letter he sent me. They were not his words at all. He was just playing the tune in order to be "a good prisoner." He had some very interesting stories to tell. Most important of all, there had been a concentrated effort to minimize that any of his experiences had anything to do with the mind control operation at Montauk.

This is the story of how I came to know Stewart Swerdlow. His very existence seemed to leak out of the government's mind control infrastructure. This book will also show how he came across Duncan Cameron, Preston Nichols, and Al Bielek. But, there is another interesting point I would like to add about Stewart.

Before I met him, Duncan always described Stewart as being a more advanced psychic than himself. Using his own metaphysical terminology, Duncan says that most people walking around the street are "sevens," meaning they have an auric lattice structure within their magnetic field that manifests itself as seven pieces of a puzzle (seven chakras, etc.). Duncan himself says that he is a "fourteen," meaning he has a double lattice. Stewart, according to Duncan, is a "twenty-one," meaning he has a triple lattice.

Duncan explained to me that a "twenty-one" represents a "bleed through" effect from higher dimensions into physical reality. This accounts for strange or paranormal phenomena that you may hear, read about, or experience directly yourself. The idea is that all manifest reality is the result of an apriori consciousness which created or determined matter, energy, space, and time in the first place.

If mind control researchers were looking for an ideal subject to explore the hidden realms of the collective unconscious, Stewart would have been a perfect candidate. His experiences prove that. It is with the above perspective in mind that we should embrace the following book. Not every one of Stewart's remarkable experiences can be documented to have occurred in physical reality, but many have left undeniable traces than can be verified. More importantly, he is a remarkably intelligent and gifted individual who has intriguing insights into the realm of the unconscious. His incredible story offers a new glimpse at the secrets of space and time and the consciousness which regulates such. Even more important, he has a priceless legacy to share.

1

THE PHILADELPHIA EXPERIMENT

Aboard the steel grey ship, sailors rushed about with anticipation and concern. They had been told that they were part of a secret exercise that would be decisive in the outcome of the war in Europe and Asia. Some of the men were volunteers, others had been assigned. All were told that, if successful, they would go down in history as the men who saved America and the world.

Anchored in the center of the harbor and away from public view, the ship was sheltered from the scrutiny of other naval vessels at the base. Many engineers and scientists were busy finalizing the connections of some very strange equipment in the control center on the top deck. At a nearby dock, a land-based control center was filled with scientific observers from the highest echelons of government. Communication between this center and the ship was constant.

Johannes von Gruber slipped aboard without any fanfare and went directly to the control room where the equipment was now ready. He observed the young sailors stationed at designated locations in preparation for what was about to begin. He thought, "If they knew the real mission of this ship, they would all think twice about staying on board. Never before in the history of mankind has an experiment of this kind been attempted on such a grand scale with living beings. Tesla had better be right or there will be hell to pay...literally!"

His thoughts suddenly flashed back to the journey that had brought him to America. The trip had been slow and tedious. As a high-ranking naval officer decorated in World War I, von Gruber had access to many sources of false documents. These enabled him to travel in the early summer of 1943; first, by train to Switzerland to meet with some very secretive individuals, then by plane to Spain, on to Portugal, and finally the United States. His mission was personal as well as one of extreme importance to those in power behind the scenes. So secret was this journey that even his closest friends, family, and superiors were unaware of the event. If he failed to return for any reason, all would be told that he had perished in the raging war.

No longer in his uniform of the Third Reich, a glance at his U.S. issue khakis and black boots jolted him back to his present reality. The implications of the experiment were foremost in his mind. In previous tests, small objects became invisible for a few seconds. True, some lab animals failed to return to visibility, but these kinks had allegedly been corrected. First, the scientists would render the ship, the *USS Eldridge*, completely invisible, then return it to a normal state. Next, they would actually attempt to transport the entire ship, crew and all, to a distant location — probably in Norfolk Harbor. Such an accomplishment would eliminate war on Earth because whoever controlled this technology would be invincible. The major governments of the world — the United States, Germany, Britain, Russia, and France — would then band together to eliminate the lesser powers and races of the

Earth. Then, they planned to beam vast conquering armies anywhere in the universe they desired. The new world government would rule the known universe! For this, the Reich was willing to unite with the United States. Because of the contacts that the Reich had with a certain group of "visitors," the United States was also willing to lay aside ideological differences. Each side believed that it would eventually control the entire plan.

At the designated time, the equipment was turned on at low power. After a slight shudder, lights blinked on the ship and at the land base. Everything glowed a mild green. Johannes felt an electric current flow up his spine and a sensation of nausea. He then watched as orders were sent from the land base to increase to full power and complete the experiment. The ship's public address system broadcast an alert for all hands to remain at their stations until the experiment was completed.

Scientists on the land base watched as electric sparks flew from the ship. The vessel turned a mustard yellow, then a bright green, and finally a dark electric blue as it disappeared into hyperspace. At that same moment, cameras on land recorded two unidentified flying objects hovering above the ship. As the ship faded from sight, they both disappeared.

On board the *Eldridge*, von Gruber felt waves of energy pour through and around him. Even though he felt the floor beneath his feet, there was a sensation of falling. Blue, green, and ultraviolet colors surrounded him. A loud crackling noise sounded like a transformer sparking. As the entire ship took on a dreamlike quality, he heard men yelling and screaming. The metal structure itself appeared to waver as if it was part of an ocean. Johannes finally focused away from his own thoughts and looked around. He saw ship hands running as others screamed orders, their voices muffled as if underwater. Johannes saw the panels on the equipment going wildly out of control. Slowly, he moved out of the control room.

Looking through a doorway, shock overcame him. Instead of a harbor, he saw electric, pulsating energy fields of color, swirling lights, and a couple of strange-looking crafts floating nearby. Von Gruber saw sailors screaming and jumping overboard. He yelled for them to stop, but either they did not hear him, or just did not pay attention. As their bodies went over the railing, they seemed to disappear into the energy streams.

Looking back into the control room, he saw men trying to destroy the equipment with sledgehammers. He also saw the horrific sight of sailors actually sinking into the metal flooring as if nothing was solid anymore. Everything appeared to be fluid energy. This was so frightening to Johannes that he panicked. If he stayed on deck, the ship might explode or turn into pure energy; if he jumped overboard, he might cease to exist. He then thought of his wife and children in Germany. They would never know what happened to him. He also thought of his superiors in the secret organizations. They had never told him that this could happen. To hell with their cause and to hell with this lunatic experiment. Over the side he went.

At first, it felt as if he were flying fast through the air. A loud whooshing was accompanied by an ever-present crackling sound. Johannes thought that he was now dying. A great peace came over him as he no longer felt his body, just the electric sensations. He started to hear ringing in his ears. As it got louder, he felt a sensation of pressure all around him as his body began to take form again. His cells tingled. The colors turned to grey as he felt something hard under his feet. The grey started to take form, and more natural shapes and colors appeared in front of him.

Dizzy and confused, he did not know where he was. He saw dark water surrounded by rocks and stone. Looking down, he realized that he stood on a hard walkway located on a catwalk bordering the dark water. Above was rock. This was some kind of indoor pool or perhaps a manmade cave. Although it was well lit, he saw no fixtures.

Suddenly, three figures ran toward him from a cutrock staircase that led up a narrow slope along the wall. One was dressed in a dark blue military uniform with American insignia. The other two were small grey beings with large wraparound eyes. They waved long metallic-looking wands at Johannes. He wanted to scream from the sight of them, but nothing came out. He could not move but was suddenly following them up the narrow staircase to an opening in the rock wall above them. Over and over in his head, a voice repeated, "Don't be afraid; follow us." The military man followed behind them.

The next thing Johannes remembered was a dark room filled with equipment. Strapped to a chair, his head was locked into a support of some kind. Scared, he was unable to move or talk. After what seemed like hours, a small, chubby man in a green jumpsuit stood in front of him, speaking in German.

"We understand that you are frightened, but this will all be over soon. You are in an American underground installation. The location is unimportant to you now. You came here by mistake, but we are going to correct that."

Suddenly, perhaps because of something they did, Johannes was able to speak slowly.

"Where am I, please?"

"Nowhere that is of any consequence to you."

"Please let me go back to my family. I'll tell you whatever you want to know."

"Your family is dead now. This is 1960. Everything

you know is gone. Germany lost the war and all of your superiors were executed."

Johannes closed his eyes tightly and gasped. Surely this was a terrible nightmare. But, the nightmare got worse when a tall, bald being with large blue eyes entered the room and the little man left. This being was about seven-feet tall. He was very thin, had a pointed chin, and his skin was exceptionally white. The creature did not talk but communicated telepathically inside von Gruber's head.

"Do not be afraid. You are going to a more appropriate situation."

With that, the being touched some controls. What seemed like thousands of volts of electricity jolted through von Gruber's body. He shook violently for some time, then was still. He felt himself glide upward in a funnel of light where he was soon met by beautiful angelic beings who gently took his hands. The rest is all a blur. There was a review of his life, a glimpse of his past lives, a period of mourning for all the wrong that he had done, and a happy feeling for all of the good that he had accomplished. Then he was told he had to complete something on Earth. He was shown a woman in labor in a brand new hospital. The next thing he knew, he was inside a tube of light heading toward her.

2

A STRANGE CHILDHOOD

Eleanor had gone into labor with her first child later than anticipated. At the hospital, she waited many hours in pain as women who came after her delivered their children and left. Aggravated and worried, she was finally examined by her physician. He said that she needed surgery before her baby could be born. In fact, her birth canal was almost completely sealed shut. The doctors were baffled about how she became pregnant in the first place! It was almost a miracle. She was transported to a new wing of the hospital that had not yet opened to the public. Even though it was early November, the heating system was not yet installed. That day, a specialist just happened to be visiting the hospital. This doctor would assist with the delivery. Extremely cold, she was grateful when they put her out.

Because the baby's neck was somehow hooked around his mother's pelvic bone, the doctors used forceps to carefully disconnect his head from her hip. They then maneuvered him down the newly formed birth canal that they had just surgically created. When I finally emerged into the world on November 5, 1956, I was already bruised and battered. I weighed in at 8 pounds, 12 ounces.

The first president of the Soviet Union was my great-uncle, Yakov Sverdlov. He was a leader and orator of the new Bolshevik movement. When Czar Nicholas was in power, he imprisoned Yakov in Siberia to try to squelch the uprisings. There, he became the cellmate of Stalin. Because of his imprisonment, Yakov developed a seething hatred for the Czar and all that he represented. When the royal family was finally cornered in the Ural mountain city of Yekaterinburg, Yakov ordered the execution of the Czar and his family. In gratitude, the new Communist government renamed the city of their assassination Sverdlovsk. In Russian, this means "the city of Swerdlow." After the fall of Communism in 1989, it was renamed Yekaterinburg. The province encompassing the city is still called Sverdlovsk. This is the homeland of current leader Boris Yeltsin. The newly independent country of Ukraine has renamed an eastern city Sverdlovsk. In Moscow, there is also a Sverdlov square.

My grandfather helped form the Communist party in the United States in the 1930's. During World War II, it was believed that my father's mother spied for the USSR in Europe against the Germans. When I was born, my father was just out of the army where he had worked on some top secret projects for the government in the American southwest. He underwent extensive interrogations by the military before he was allowed to work on these projects. I often wondered why they considered him in the first place. Now I realize that, because my father is a brilliant engineer, the government probably wanted to be sure of his loyalty. My father almost never talks about his parents or his family background. Much of what I have learned about my great-uncle Yakov Sverdlov came from reading Russian history books.

My mother is a sweet, generous, caring woman devoted to her family. Her mother ran around central Europe with Gypsy caravans travelling through the area.

When my grandmother was a little girl in Austria, she was playing outside with two cousins when she glanced up and saw the image of a man who looked exactly like the Jack of Spades in playing cards. Quickly, she told her cousins to look up at it. Immediately, they fell dead to the ground. Shortly after that incident, my grandmother was sent to America to live with relatives. Amazingly, nearly a century later, I was involved with a group of government related individuals who were trying to understand the meaning of a message from hyperspace. Beamed from outside the Earth, the message was an image of a being who resembled the Jack of Spades!

As a child, I saw the spirits of dead people hanging around apartments and other people. Constant ringing filled my ears. Colors flashed before my open eyes, and I saw fragments of future scenes that always came to pass. Plagued with nightmares, my parents spent more time sleeping in my room to comfort me than they did in their own bed. I was a moody and frightened child. Although brilliant in school, I found it slow-paced and boring. Usually I stayed home pretending to be sick, entertaining myself with psychic and mental games. Practically friendless, I found people my own age to be childish and stupid. Instead, I preferred the company of adults, particularly the elderly. For some reason, I enjoyed hearing stories about the old days, especially the 1930's and 1940's. I loved watching war movies, but I was ashamed to tell anyone that I always privately cheered for the Germans because my background is Jewish. Interestingly enough, I also cheered for the Indians in Western movies.

Alien beings routinely pursued me in my childhood nightmares. After capturing and examining me, they indoctrinated me, feeding me vast amounts of information. Even though I was afraid of them, I always wanted the aliens to win in the science-fiction films and television shows that I enjoyed watching. I am sure that there are some therapists who would have a field day with this. The standard diagnosis is that I was probably abused, and the repressed fear and anger came out in my nightmares. Despite this, four separate therapists, all unknown to one another, have pronounced me completely sane and have determined that I am not the victim of abuse.

I always say that I never had a childhood—I was born an adult. I never felt like a child nor did I ever want to play games or participate in parties and whatever else children do. Whenever I tried to explain my daily and nightly experiences to others, I was ridiculed or told that I was imagining it. After awhile, I kept the information to myself and turned into a very private little boy who was unhappy. Teachers wrote on my report cards, "intelligent, but never smiles." I always thought, "Why should I smile when I know the terrible things that are going to happen on this Earth?"

As a child, I had problems with my eyesight and hearing. After testing me, the doctors found nothing wrong. Even so, they gave me glasses and hoped to improve me by taking out my tonsils and adenoids. It did not work. In fact, I am still hard of hearing and my sight is atrocious. However, I do see auras and the archetypes and symbols that emanate from people's mind-patterns. I also hear tones.

My worst childhood memories are of what are commonly called "alien abductions." While I now know that a few of those experiences actually happened, others were hyperspace experiences, and many were government generated. I vividly remember the terror of being removed from my bed in the middle of the night by small beings wearing dark bodysuits who never spoke a word out loud.

As a child, I was afraid to go to sleep at night because I feared that they might take me away forever, performing those painful tests on my body. They always told me that I was related to them; that some time in the future they would keep me with them. Although I did not particularly care for the Earth and its cruel population, I loved my family and did not want to leave them. I remember asking, even pleading, with these beings to let me go home. They obviously always did. Still, I never trusted them.

Wherever they took me, it was always cold. Because there were only a couple of times that I actually saw that I was not on the Earth, I cannot say for sure that I was on board a spacecraft. Coldhearted and unfeeling toward me, the beings did what they had to do before returning me. I have several memories of descending rapidly in an elevator. At our destination, I saw human men moving about in dark blue uniforms without insignia. Some were armed; some herded other children and adults to various rooms in this complex. Windowless, all the walls and floors were smooth and polished. Small vehicles silently moved through narrow corridors. A few times, I was in cavernous spaces stacked with boxes or supplies of some sort. Since then, I have always hated being in large warehouses. Once, I remember escaping from my holding pen or room and running naked through the hallways. I hid under a table in a small room. Several of the above-mentioned men came looking for me. When they found me, I passed out from fear.

The most spectacular event in my life occurred when I was about six-years old. I remember being aboard a small craft that flew through the air. Tiny and dark silver, it was shaped like a round room inside with a small ladder that went up to a domed room. That was all there was to this craft. With me was a greenish-grey creature with a heart-shaped head and round, black eyes. Almost exactly my height, it wore no clothing and had only four fingers on each hand. Its small feet ended in two equal length toes. The creature's wet skin felt like a corn husk. Speaking mentally, but slowly, it showed me a window on the wall as it directed me to look outside. I saw that we were above the clouds. Not far away flew two or three other crafts identical to ours. The atmosphere in the craft was humid and thick. Even though I did not feel hot, I was perspiring. As I followed the creature up the ladder to the domed room, the dome suddenly became transparent. I felt like we were flying on the roof of the craft without any walls around us!

Travelling at an incredible speed, I felt my skin tighten and crawl. My nose burned, my eyes watered, and I felt extremely nauseous. Every now and then, the craft slowed down and I found myself some place else over the Earth. Low enough to see the landscape clearly, I remember flying over a large ocean, then seeing large cities through dissipating clouds. I now know one of these cities was Paris. Another one was Rome, then Athens. I saw the pyramids in Egypt, and a vast desert. There were tremendous snow-capped mountains below that I believe were the Himalayas. I remember travelling slowly over a beautiful and varied countryside resembling India, then China, and then Japan. Sometimes, the name of the place flashed in my mind as we flew over it. Other times, it was simply identified on a global map that I saw inside my head. Alaska and Antarctica were the most thrilling places because I have an affinity for icy and snowy locales, but more will be said about that later.

I was told that we circled the globe three times west to east, then three times north to south. There was a particular reason for this and for seeing the places that I was shown. Finally, as we started to move straight up, I told the creature that I wanted to go home. Still in my pajamas, I did not want my parents to miss me. There was no reply, but we ascended so quickly that I fell to the floor feeling very sick. The craft finally seemed to be flying slowly. Suddenly, I saw the Earth through the transparent wall. Dark outside, there were no stars in the sky. The moon looked huge. A bright round globe in the distance was our sun, I was told. Commanded to turn and face the other wall, I was amazed to see that we were approaching a gigantic dark metallic platform floating in space. Various types of ships were all around it and on it. Some ships were disk-shaped and others looked like globes, but the strangest ones resembled tubes and triangles. I could not keep my eyes open as a terrific sleepiness fell over me. I realized that I could not move.

When I woke up, I was floating in the air in a brightly lit place. Standing and floating around me in a circle were beings of every species possibly imaginable. Slowly, I descended to the floor. My heart pounded, but I was not afraid. The fear came later when I realized that I was not dreaming! At that point, my education began.

3

THE MENAGERIE

Standing in the center of a circle, I was surrounded by a vast array of every conceivable type of being. The most beautiful and imposing of all was a gigantic butterfly. It seemed to float in midair in front of a huge window, through which I saw the Earth. In my child's mind, I thought that this must be a magical dreamland. Too excited to be afraid, my mouth hung open at the awesome sight before me. After a few minutes, the thoughts of these beings flooded my mind. Sounding like gibberish, I telepathically heard a kind of mixed hum. Slowly, I realized that I could tune into each individual being's stream of thinking.

I concentrated on the butterfly first because it seemed so magnificent. I wanted to hang in the air just like it did. At first, the butterfly seemed startled that I chose it instead of another being. Its surprise startled me, too! I had thought that it wanted to talk to me. In the background, I heard/sensed the others vying for my attention. They suddenly stopped when they observed my desire to communicate with the butterfly.

As I approached the window and the wondrous creature, I did not feel my feet move. I merely thought of getting closer, and I did! The room was intensely cold, but for some reason, I was able to tolerate it. I suppose that I was in a state of shock. Finally, the butterfly spoke to me telepathically. I did not hear words, but I knew what it said. Because our language patterns were so different, it was difficult for it to talk to me, it said. As it tried very hard to translate my thoughts and reply in a way that I could understand, it told me that it was neither male nor female, nor did it have a name as I did. Instead, each member of its species was identified by the others through the tone of its individual frequency. At the beginning of Earth's history, this butterfly's species donated DNA for Project Earth to create the creatures on Earth known as butterflies. Continuing, it said that the butterflies on Earth monitor magnetism and know how to adjust it so that it has a beneficial effect on the environment. Moths were created as a negative aspect of this by the dark side. For every good thing that was created on Earth, the dark side made an opposite to counter it.

The butterfly told me that its species does not create spaceships for themselves. If they need to venture outside of their planetary system, they travel with another humanoid group. Lush and green, the butterfly's home planet has flowers in colors that do not exist on Earth. Their planet is located in a distant sector of this galaxy, but their species had been taken to populate other worlds in other universes that were more suited to their needs. No matter where in the universe they exist, they communicate within their species at will. They have little physical contact with other species outside of their home worlds but enjoy telepathically sending spiritual messages to humanoids. In some cases, they even "adopt" a humanoid as a spiritual student. That is why it had come to this meeting. Apparently, I was its student! Finally, it said that it was time for me to communicate with the other beings, but it wanted me to know that for the rest of my stay on Earth, it would send Monarch butterflies to greet and comfort me. Whenever I saw a white butterfly at an opportune moment, there was a message for me. As the grand butterfly communicated with me, pulsating glows emanated from its beautiful wings.

Suddenly, I turned and faced the other members of this strange gathering. Tears began to run down my face. The next creature to communicate with me was a huge, white praying mantis. As it came closer to me, I froze with fear. Trying to scream, nothing came out. The mantis emitted a loud and constant clicking and chirping that completely unnerved me. I could not stand its presence. Sensing this, it immediately backed away. The mantis was not evil or negative. It was simply an unconventional (non-humanoid) mind-pattern. Insect species are truly alien in perception and context of our reality.

The next being to stand in front of me was about five-feet tall with a large cone-shaped head. Wearing a long silver-grey robe, its moist skin appeared to match the color of the robe. The large, octopus-like eyes were dull and black. There was no visible nose, and the mouth was fishlike. I immediately understood that it was amphibious and needed to return to water soon. Telepathically, the creature told me that he was a male and that my DNA had marine origins. He seemed kind as he informed me that someday I would be aware of this.

The next thing that I remember is becoming dizzy and nauseous. Falling to the floor, I awoke sitting in a chair facing a panel of seven beings. Much too big for me, the chair seemed like a throne. The sides of the chair were as high as my shoulders, not allowing my feet to touch the ground. As each being spoke to me, my chair automatically swivelled to face the speaker.

Speaking in succession from right to left, the first one was a large reptilian creature who looked like a lizard stuffed into a black uniform. He spoke with a hissing noise in a language that sounded guttural and severe. Simultaneously, I heard the meaning of his words in my head. A member of a vast empire that spanned a large portion of the galaxy, his people are attempting to occupy all of the star systems on the outer fringes of this galaxy, eventually working their way inward. A defector, he now advises this council on the possible activities of these invasion forces.

According to the lizard, the Earth was invaded many thousands of years ago by an army of his people that arrived in a huge ship that is now the moon of Earth. Another such ship is on its way, he said, destined to arrive before the end of this century (as we calculate time). After being driven off the Earth by settlers from the Lyraen Empire, his people went underground. There, they remain in stasis until they are to be reactivated by the incoming ship. These reptilians also maintain bases on Venus and on some of the moons of the outer planets. Because his people are male only, they created females for the sole purpose of breeding. Despite this, cloning is their primary method of reproduction. In conclusion, the lizard added that I would someday convert his people to the Light because my soul was an emissary to them many years ago. Remembering me, they would respect what I said to them.

The next one to speak was an amphibian-type being who looked very much like the "Creature from the Black Lagoon." Slimy and moist, his body was covered with a scaly, greenish-grey skin. Breathing heavily, his thoughts flooded my brain. His civilization was the original inhabitant of Earth before the others arrived. At that time, Earth was mostly water and marshes. Devastated by mankind and aliens alike, there remain only a few pockets of his people at the deepest depths of the oceans. From time to time they come to dry land to sun themselves, thus creating the basis for the legendary mermaids and mermen. This species worked closely with the Atlanteans before that continent sank. They served as liaisons between mankind and the whales and dolphins. He said that these sea mammals are advanced races from another galaxy. Most of his people were lifted off-world to underground oceans on Neptune. This maneuver was facilitated by benevolent ET groups. Continuing, he told me that I have dolphin DNA; therefore, I could learn to communicate with his species in order to help mankind and the dolphin/whale systems.

Next, a being on the opposite side of the table spoke. Looking like a small dark-haired human, his eyes were so dark that they almost shined. His eyes seemed to pierce right through my own, and I found it difficult to look at him. Claiming to represent the Federation of Planets of this galaxy, he said that there are over 120 different member civilizations. Someday, Earth will be asked to join, but only if they are successful in repelling the invasion force. Otherwise, Earth could become a target by the Federation until the reptilians are removed.

This dark-haired human said that I was selected to speak with all of these aliens because each species had contributed to my DNA creation. I was made for the express genetic purpose of belonging to many different groups. Because of that, each group would be more willing to listen to me and accept my ideas since I partially belonged to them. Continuing, he said that my soul-personality had agreed to this mission long ago, undergoing training in many galaxies and alternate universes. He said that much of what they told me now would stay hidden in my cellular memory until each piece of information becomes necessary. Future hardships and sadness would condition me for my mission. Not wanting to hear any of this, I tensed up to the point of vomiting. The next thing I remember, I was still in the chair with another being talking to me.

This creature was a pale greyish-white. He possessed large, round, black eyes and a long nose. A short "curtain" of material draped around the back of his large head. His thin mouth did not move as he spoke words inside my head. With a harsh attitude, this "grey" claimed to be from the Rigel star system. Although he did not want to be part of this meeting, his overlords insisted that he attend it. His job was to monitor the procedures since I was once a part of their race, too. His home world was once part of the Lyraen civilization. After that culture disintegrated, the reptilians invaded his planet. Now his people are part of that empire and as such, do their bidding. From time to time he would send his workers, smaller grey creatures, to check up on me. Most of the time I would not remember it except as a bad dream.

There would come a time when these greys would be at war with some of the worlds represented at this meeting. My job would then be to monitor the activities and report the findings to my controllers. My body contains chemicals needed by his race. The grey said that his race also looked human until war contaminated their environment, genetically degenerating them. My body was presented to them as a temporary token of hope and peace. Allowed to use my genetics for the purpose of upgrading their dying species, they could not purposefully harm me, permanently kidnap me, or allow me to remember what they did to get what they needed from me. These were the rules that all abided by to keep the status quo while at the same time benefiting from my creation.

If my mission failed, or if any of the participants in this project no longer wished to continue, then I would be removed to a safe place while the others fought amongst themselves, possibly even on the surface of the planet Earth. Finally, he told me that his people merely wished to correct the errors committed against them in order to evolve. They wished to become independent of the reptilians and recreate their old civilization before it was too late. Their dilemma was that, if they attempted this, they would be destroyed completely by their masters. On the other hand, if they continued with their masters' orders, they would be targeted by the Federation planets. Because they felt hopeless, they looked out only for themselves.

At this point, the last being at the council table, who sat in the middle, interrupted the Rigelian. This being was very tall. Standing up, he raised his arms to either side. The beautiful white robe he wore was trimmed in a blue that I had never seen before. His large head was round on top with a pointed chin. Standing with his arms outstretched, he remarkably resembled a living ankh. His oval eyes were brilliant blue; his skin ivory white. By far, he was the most impressive being at this gathering. When his thoughts filled my head, I could not even think of my own name! As he spoke, I saw words in a strange language swirling ethereally around his head.

He told me his name, but I cannot remember it. Coming from the planet Khoom in the binary Sirius star system, his people were descendents of nonphysical beings who inhabited hyperspace, a region of consciousness existing outside of linear time and space. They created the ancient Egyptian civilization as well as the Jewish people and gave them the Torah. The Crystal Skull was their creation, and they were in charge of many events in the galaxy and beyond. My soul-personality was from his people because it was the only type advanced enough to animate such a hybrid body as my own. Possessing the most advanced technology in the universe, all the other species came to these Sirians for information. Now, as an adult, I realize that this group also plays one civilization against the other to benefit evolution as well as their own species.

As I got older, he continued, more and more of my memories would return to me; not only of this particular event, but from my existences in other star systems and universes. I would be a teacher of untold races and species. However, within me was also a program of self-destruction that would eliminate my mission forever. He said that I could not possibly understand the meaning of my mission at this time but that was as it should be. This way, I could not tamper with it or my programming. Many would try to deceive me; even those I considered to be my closest allies. This Sirian said he would always be there to guide me, stating that our soul-personalities were connected in a way that I would understand when I was much older. Only after several segments of my alternate selves come together would the heart of my mission begin. Until then my situation would, at times, be precarious. Again, the reasons would not become apparent for a long time.

This large Sirian began to glow a white light with violet, gold, and silver overtones. He then faded into the center of this light. Next, I woke up screaming in my bed at home and felt a terror beyond my imagination. The screams woke my baby sister, and my parents ran into my room to see if someone was trying to kill me. After a long while, I finally caught my breath; but I would not let my parents leave my room. Even though I wanted to, I could not tell them what I had experienced. The words would just not come out.

For many years thereafter, I had repeated nightmares about that event. With each bad dream, I remembered more and more information. Gradually, within two years of the experience, I began to see images of dead people around the living. I also received information in my head about the state of health of any person in front of me. Simply by hearing only the name of a person, I could tune into that person's state of being and give an accurate description of his or her well-being.

The nightmares became more intense as I got older, as did my preoccupation with UFO's and aliens. Something compelled me to watch every science-fiction movie and television show possible. I also read as much about space exploration as I could. Intuitively, I knew if a particular story was true or false.

My frustration grew as I realized that there was absolutely no one on the face of the Earth with whom I could converse. Invariably, I wanted to speak about my knowledge of what lay beyond physical reality but was afraid of others' reactions. In those days (the late 50's and 60's), UFO's were still considered to be from the land of the mentally ill.

By the time I reached puberty, more than just my body changed. My nightly experiences took on an even stranger aura. Almost every night, I felt my consciousness lift out of my body and enter a room of bright light where I was intensely instructed. Topics ranged from my origins, to the nature of physical reality, and to the possibilities of time travel. I always came back to my body before dawn and woke up extremely exhausted and uncomfortable. It was as if I had walked fifty miles nonstop. Feeling too tired to want to go to school, I played hooky often enough to have the truant officer pay me a visit a couple of times. Whenever I was in school, I found the entire process boring. I was way ahead of my classmates in every subject and felt as if they weighed me down and held me back. My mind constantly wandered to the stars, where I knew my real home existed. The Earth was as alien to me as the farthest star in the galaxy would be to a human being. I did not like other people, nor did I act or think in the same ways. A complete loner, my parents tried ceaselessly to involve me with other children. But to me, arrogant as it may sound, the thought of playing stupid games with other children was repulsive when I could be working on ways to improve the NASA space program.

Night after night, I begged the star people to come and take me away forever. Why did I have to stay on this primitive planet? Although I was afraid of the experience when the aliens came, there was something about being with them that made me feel comfortable and at peace. Then one night, when I was about eleven-years old, I had another interesting experience.

Waking up in the middle of the night in my bedroom, I had an eerie feeling of being watched. A cold shudder went down my entire body as I tried to scream out for my parents, but nothing came out of my mouth. The next thing I knew, three small greyish-white aliens were in my room. Suddenly, I shifted to a standing position and flew right out through the closed window. Immediately, I was in a small metallic-grey room with one of the aliens standing next to me. On the wall, I saw a screen with a conveyor belt beneath it. Openings in the wall allowed the ends of the conveyor belt to pass through. Telepathically, the little grey being asked me to watch the pictures on the screen, correlating them to food that would soon pass in front of me on the conveyor belt.

Asked to identify the pictures with the food, I was directed to say whether or not I would ever eat it. The screen then displayed a picture of a moving rhinoceros. Simultaneously, the conveyor belt started to move carrying a slab of meat, which I understood to be from a rhinoceros. I remember thinking, "Absolutely not!" Then, a picture of a cow appeared on the screen as a steak slid out on the moving conveyor belt. I thought, "Yes," and immediately, the taste of the meat was in my mouth—uncooked! This series of pictures and meat went on for quite some time. There were chickens, goats, elephants, insects, worms, birds, sea life, and plants.

Eventually, I began to get tired and sick to my stomach. The small being turned off the screen, escorting me abruptly back to my room. As strange as it sounds, he took me through the walls of the ship and my bedroom simultaneously. As I was literally thrust back onto my bed, I felt that they were angry with me for not completing the test or whatever it was that they were doing. Morning was only minutes away. I was really sick, but after so many times of telling my mother that I could not go to school, I forced myself to get up. The memory of the experience haunted me for days afterwards. I could not stop thinking of the images on the screen, realizing that the aliens had killed these creatures in order to get the meat. This nauseated me most of all. My horror grew even stronger when I remembered that the last image on the screen before I got sick was a picture of a man!

4

PUBERTY

My teenage years were typical by all outward appearances, but my private life continued to be extraordinary. My abductions increased to two or three times each week. Now, I realize that these were not always physical abductions. In fact, actual physical abductions only occurred two or three times each year. The rest of the times were astral, taking only my spirit for instruction and indoctrination.

Usually, I went to sleep in my bed and "woke up" in a small metallic room where everything seemed constructed of a single piece without seams or lines of any kind. The room had rounded ends with benches facing a curved wall and a ceiling that connected directly to the floor. Always naked, I sat with other human beings on these benches. As pictures appeared with colors and symbols, they were accompanied with verbal instructions that manifested from a voice behind us.

Most of our learning centered around specific circumstances such as our role in Earth's future. We seemed to be some kind of army or brigade programmed to perform certain functions at a particular time. The functions were not to be remembered until they were needed. In my heart, I felt that this was a negative programming, but I did not know how to get rid of it. The fact that I had such terrible things inside of myself scared me, especially because I did not know what they were. After several hours of these instructions, we all stood up, turned around, and waited to be escorted to our homes.

My family moved from Brooklyn to Suffolk County, Long Island when I was thirteen-years old. Being away from the congestion and hostility of the city gave me a sense of freedom. We moved on a cold day in the middle of winter. The huge house had many places to be alone. Finally, I had a private room with my own closet. A large, wooded back yard separated the house from a drive-in movie theater. When the leaves were gone from the trees in the winter, I could actually watch the movies from a second floor window. I remember watching *Midnight Cowboy* with Dustin Hoffman and Jon Voight in 1970. My sister and I laughed at the sexual scenes. This caused my parents to yell at us from downstairs, but that only made us laugh even more.

The first few weeks were not too bad in the new house. My dreams were normal except for one thing. I often went to bed wearing pajamas and covered with a blanket, but woke up naked with the blanket on the floor. At other times, I projected out of my body and floated through the house in what seemed to be another dimension where everything glowed and pulsated.

Several times, I had a series of recurring nightmares. In these dreams, I ran away from uniformed men in what appeared to be a large warehouse without any windows. I always hid under a table in a small room that led to a corridor. The men then burst through the door, looked around without finding me, and left to continue their search. After that, I crawled out from under the table just as another group of uniformed men came through the door and captured me. I would start to scream and wake up in my bed gasping for air. Whenever I woke up from these nightmares and looked at my bedroom window, I saw the face of a blond man surrounded by red light. I always screamed, and as I did, the man would start to laugh at me. The louder I screamed, the harder he laughed. I felt all the energy drain out of my body. Invariably, my mother ran into my room to find out what happened to me. When I looked at the window again, the face was always gone. This went on for years. The haunting thing about it was that I felt as if I knew this man in my window. I almost felt that he was my friend or even a relative I could not place.

On other occasions, worse things happened. At least once or twice each month, I woke up in a strange cold room. Naked, I was paralyzed and unable to speak. Small grey beings were always around the table or platform on which I lay. They refused to respond to my thoughts or fearful looks. Sometimes, a voice spoke in my mind and told me it would soon be over and that I would not remember a thing. The problem was that I remembered everything. They always had a tube going into the tip of my penis, which was usually erect, as well as something very tight on my testicles and nipples. On some occasions, a tube or hose went into my rectum. All of it was extremely painful, and I always had tears in my eyes.

These beings were cold and unfeeling. One of them once told me that I was part of their project and that I knew about it and had agreed to it. Basically, he told me to shut up since I was one of their co-workers. At the end of these experiences, I felt myself painfully ejaculate. I always thought that blood was coming out of me. Then they removed the tubes and probes, making me lie on that cold table for a long while in silence. Next, one of them examined my eyes, nose, and ears. Long, outrageous-looking objects were put high up into my nostrils. On these occasions, I always came back to my bed with a nose hemorrhage. At one point, my parents took me to a specialist to cauterize my nostrils and wash my ears out. This still did not stop the bleeding. Every time the greys took me, I had some sort of physical reaction. Much of the time, my eyes were irritated since they occasionally put what appeared to be contact lenses in my eyes. One time, they removed a large gelatinous mass from deep in my throat. When I saw them remove it, I immediately threw up.

These experiences produced an interesting emotional effect on me as a teenager — I had a deep longing for children. This is not what one would expect from a teenage boy! I constantly felt that I was a father who missed his children. I did not know who they were, where they were, or if they even existed. My logical mind told me that it could in no way be true, but my emotions persisted.

When I was seventeen, my feelings came to a realization. Waking up inside a typical ship, if indeed that was where they took me, I found myself sitting on a chair fully clothed. This was strange because, until now, I was always naked, paralyzed, and lying down. Around me were little greys and a tall blond being in a blue uniform. In the background were two human males dressed in military uniforms. They appeared to be observers while the tall blond seemed to direct the entire situation.

After a few minutes, the greys took me from the chair and led me to a small room with different lighting. There, I was shown a tiny infant cradled by another grey with female characteristics. This surprised me since they always said that they were neither male nor female as we know it. Perhaps she was a hybrid of some sort.

As the grey put the baby in my arms, I realized that it felt practically weightless. I just stared at its drawn, boney face, noticing that its skin was pasty and pale. Its dark, slightly almond-shaped eyes stared back from its hairless, elongated head, yet it did not make a sound. Knowing that it was too weak to make any noise or even move, sadness for the poor thing filled my heart. I was then told that it was my child and that my genetics had produced several such infants. Some had died, but the stronger ones were removed to another location on a safe world, whatever that meant. The greys wanted to know if sick babies respond to their parents' touch, especially the human ones, and if a bonding would occur. I remember feeling happy that I had this child, but I felt anger at the same time because it was sick and not human. I could never tell anyone about it, nor could I ever assist with its upbringing or education.

The tall blond appeared to be pleased with this meeting and the infant was immediately removed from the room. I asked if it would live and if I could see it again. I even asked if I could permanently stay with the child. My questions went unanswered as I was promptly returned home. Waking in tears several hours later, my longing for my offspring was stronger than ever.

Shortly after this last encounter, my habits changed. Suddenly, I felt the need to maintain my body in top-notch condition. I began a regimen of heavy daily exercise coupled with fasting several times each week. Refusing any food with the slightest fat content, I only ate once a day and drank lots of water. My routine also included frequent sun baths when the weather was warm. My eyes started to feel as if they were being used as cameras. Whenever I looked at something of interest, I could almost feel another consciousness looking through my eyes at the same time. I even turned my head as if it were a camera panning a scene. This other pair of eyes in my head was particularly interested in travel inside moving vehicles, shopping in malls and department stores, and was absolutely fascinated with wintery scenes. Whenever snow fell, my eyes scanned the landscape for every minute detail of the patterns and colors of the environment. Sensing that the owner(s) of the other eyes had difficulty operating in the cold and snow, I intuitively knew that my eyes provided a first-hand view that would otherwise be impossible for them to obtain. I wondered if this had something to do with my diminished eyesight. Was something put into my eyeballs which allowed others to see through them? Or, did they observe using only their mental capacities? When I finally asked, I was told that they saw by mentally focusing on a small organic chip implanted in the cornea of both eyes. Yes, they coldly responded, this might cause my natural vision to diminish. They were not very compassionate.

During one of my subsequent abductions, I was seated in a room with my back to a silver-grey wall. There was nothing else in the room except a small grey standing to my left. All of a sudden, the wall behind me became a giant screen which projected all of my thoughts into movie form. I did not know if they were downloading everything that was observed through my eyes or if they were screening my thoughts. I played with them to test it out. Thinking of a horse, the image suddenly changed to a galloping horse. This seemed to annoy my grey companion as he sharply reprimanded me to stop.

Obviously, my mind affected this device. Becoming aware of scenes of my childhood and from what appeared to be my future, I realized that this exercise was a life reading based on my mind-patterns. They were recording where I had been in life and where I was headed. This scared me because I wondered if they would change my future to suit them instead of what was best for me. This same abduction experience occurred several times before it abruptly stopped. Either they got all of the information that they needed to receive, or they reprogrammed my life in a way that was beneficial to them. I do not know which was the case.

The abductions continued for the rest of my teen years and into my twenties. Most of the time, they were for genetic reasons; but there were occasions when I was indoctrinated, used for energy draining (i.e., using my bodily energies for their own use), or sometimes simply interrogated. The most heinous aspect of the greys involved what they wanted me to do to other human children. This particularly increased in the early to mid-70's.

I was taken to a place that I discerned to be underground because of the rock walls and dampness that permeated much of that environment. Sometimes, I saw water on the floors or walls. There were never any windows, but there was always a sound. It was the terrifying sound of screaming children.

5

TERROR AT MONTAUK

To this day, I cannot bear the sound of crying children or frightened voices. I also have an overwhelming desire to care for all of the abandoned children of the world. Perhaps this is my way of penance; perhaps I will never get the images out of my mind. Or, perhaps this explains why I have had so many children since those awful days. Whatever the case, the story I am about to tell you is the truth as I remember it.

My memories of being part of the Montauk Project are not pleasant at all. When I was a prepubescent child, my role was one of subservience. Strapped to a table, I was examined, mentally scanned for my brainwave signature, or sexually abused in ways that stored my energetics and magnified them by computer. This went on until puberty.

As I had only tried to escape once, I was considered cooperative in the work with my adult supervisors. Additionally, I had not died from the testing and therefore I was "offered" a promotion of sorts. The administrators placed me in charge of disciplining the younger boys who were brought in, as well as preparing them for the mental and physical testing.

The preparation of the children included teaching them to implicitly obey orders, without any questions whatsoever. I taught them how to mentally focus on command so that their bodily energies could be removed by the psychic/mentalist to whom they were assigned. I instructed them on how to know what colors and symbols to mentally use to facilitate any given experiment. They were also taught how to relinquish their bodies and allow themselves to die without the innate defensive reaction of resistance inherent to all living beings.

A mentalist is different than a psychic. A psychic merely observes the blueprints of reality and reports on them. This is known as a "psychic reading." A mentalist actually goes in and manipulates the blueprint in order to create a different manifestation. This is what the government wanted. Machines and computers could easily read a blueprint for reality, but only a mind could change it.

Working with mentalists on this scale is no easy task because the anchor between the soul-personality and the body can be separated so easily with a child. Unfortunately, small male children have the proper levels of mental and physical energies necessary to boost a mentalist or psychic working on a computer. But, the desires and fears of these small children are directly opposed to this task, causing breakdowns on every level. Fear, coupled with the physical and mental strains of the work, often killed the boys.

Especially vulnerable were the preadolescents from the ages of three to twelve. Prized for their genetic material and mind-patterns, this group was considered to be pure and uncontaminated. However, their overwhelming fear combined with their yearning to return home led to scattered and disjointed energy outputs that were of no use to the scientists. In addition, they were often the targets of sexual abuse by an unscrupulous segment of project workers. Because of this, these boys often went insane and had to be terminated. There was no way that they could be returned to their families or society in that condition because their minds were fried and could not be reprogrammed. Death was the only solution. Frequently, they were simply starved to death and left to decompose in special cave-like chambers. Their remains were flushed out to sea where the marine life consumed them. On rare occasions, childless scientists and other workers who moved to other parts of the globe took a favorite boy with them, passing him off as their own son. Hair color and even fingerprints were changed.

Some of the boys were kidnapped, as was I, from the safety of their beds. In a manner that defies belief, time and space were folded to accommodate their disappearances. These boys were special in the sense that they came from families with a political or military connection to the secret government. Treated differently than the "common" boys, all were returned to their source of origin without exception.

Preprogrammed for specific purposes, we were the elite of the groups and were given unique assignments. Some of us were used to go out into the public and "tag" other boys to be picked up later for use in the Project. We apparently all had special implants in our eyes. This was alien technology and was used to relay information to our supervisors. Our minds were programmed to perform the work when we were in school, at the mall, etc., without our conscious knowledge. I often wonder how many helpless victims I designated for the experiments without even realizing that I was dooming most of them to their deaths!

I think of the stories about Dr. Mengele in the concentration camps. When the trains arrived at the work camps, Dr. Mengele stood by as the human cargo was unloaded, making determinations of who was going to live and who was going to die. He decided who would be a worker and who would be part of his bizarre experiments. Was I any different than that monster? Was not, after all, Johannes von Gruber a Nazi? Was he involved in the German version of the Montauk Project? Even today, these feelings of guilt prevent me from having a positive self-image, causing me to be overly critical of myself in a punishing way. Perhaps I am trying to make up for the evil of which I was a part.

Most of the boys were from outside of the New York area because the disappearance of so many from one single location would be too suspicious. So, the "common" boys, who were considered expendable, came from other parts of the country. Taken from families where they would not be missed as much as others, they were the children of prostitutes, drug addicts, and alcoholics, or they came from poor rural families with many children. If there was a child that they really wanted who did not fit the proper family profile, the family simply had an accident. The child was then taken with the public assumption that he was an accident victim. These accidents included cars going off embankments into rivers, fires where bodies were burned beyond recognition, and natural disasters such as tornadoes, hurricanes, and earthquakes; any place where there was a lot of damage and many people were missing and presumed dead.

On the other hand, the Project also utilized runaways and street people who were accessible and not easily missed by families. These were mostly adults that were used in the time travel part of the Project. Live human beings were needed to observe the effects of vortex influence on the body as well as to learn how to lock onto a person from various points in time and space. Children were not used for these purposes because their auric signatures were not the same as the adults, and it was adults that they ultimately planned to use in the manipulation of the time lines.

When the Montauk researchers physically took a body from a bedroom or other location, they often bent time and space so that virtually no time passed for the victim or those around him. Sometimes, they left an energy pattern in the victim's room that deterred anyone from entering the location and finding the person missing. Remember, they had no trouble using the equipment to send people to different locations in the "local present," or current time on the Earth within a specific geographic range. The researchers could already easily determine the frequency rates of vibration for any current place on the Earth. Problems only developed when they wanted to send someone off-world or to a distant past or future sight. Then, they had to play hit or miss until they tuned in properly. Adult guinea pigs were used for this. Many were lost in time and space, as they were on the *Eldridge*. Eventually, scientists were able to map the various points in time and space so that they could travel easily between them. At the more common destinations, they placed receivers to fix the signal and make the connections easier.

My role was to prepare the boys for use with the Project psychics, particularly Duncan Cameron, who was the lead mentalist throughout the experiment. Used as batteries, or boosters, for his mental energies, the creativity and imagination of a small child is without comparison. This energy was tapped, amplified, and plugged into Duncan to magnify his mind power to the point where he was able to open doorways to other dimensions, thus creating a pathway. His abilities were used to connect to hyperspace and the astral plane where all pre-physical reality materials and blueprints are stored. He then brought the information back in usable form so that technologies could be built.

The boys were often drained of energy very quickly and had to rest a lot. Whenever one of them was "burning out," a fear program was instigated to create a high adrenaline flow. This usually extended the final amounts of energy out of them until they could no longer be used. Then, their little hearts gave out, they went insane, had a stroke, or some combination of the above.

Whenever a teenage boy or young adult was used as a battery pack, sexual arousal and fear programs were combined to boost energy output. Frequently, the dead bodies of these individuals were given to the greys because they used the blood and soft body tissue as nutrients. Understand that the greys do not eat as human beings do. Instead, they require the hormones stored in various organs and tissues of other species, particularly humans, because they were created from human genetics many millennia ago.

The smaller grey races are without digestive systems. They absorb nutrients and excrete waste through the skin. After collecting various organs and body fluids, they store them in huge vats. The greys sit or swim in these vats several hours to absorb the extant nutritional energies. This fuels their bodies for several days. "Hunger" makes them particularly belligerent.

Several centuries ago, in order to avoid detection, the grey races genetically created beings who walked the Earth for them and collected body fluids for them. These creatures came to be known as vampires, incubi, and succubi. Because the heat of the sun removed the potency of the collected fluids, they avoided sunlight. In modern times, the aliens use a creature known in Latin America as the chupacabra, or goat sucker.

Some of the other alien groups who observed these experiments were strictly interested in the mind control aspects. Needing to control large groups of people, they did not wish to support a large army to do so. Particularly interested in this were the large reptilians who came from the Draco star system.

The most painful experience for me, beyond my own pain and suffering, was hearing the death screams and the cries of fear from the boys and teenagers who were burning out during the experiments. My actions were responsible for putting them in this position, yet I could do nothing to help them. I thought of the parents and relatives who would never know the truth about what happened to their child. I also considered the children who longed for their mommies and daddies. A lump would develop in my throat and on my chest. To this day, I wake up in the middle of the night gasping for air and screaming after remembering dreams of my involvement. Looking at my own sons, I vow that no one will ever put them through that. I realize that I did not control the events, nor was I in a frame of mind to stop them. But, I realize that something in my soul-personality needed to experience this, and that frightens me. I pray that God have mercy on the souls of those innocent victims, and also on the souls of the perpetrators.

6

OVERSEAS

My college days were a whirlwind of confusion. I began school at McGill University in Montreal, but I felt so uncomfortable there that I soon returned to the states. Drawn to Canada for many years, I enjoyed staying with relatives in Quebec during summer vacations. I even planned to permanently emigrate there and become a citizen. But no matter how hard I tried to permanently leave Long Island in those days, some strong longing always brought me back.

Finally, I wound up at a local college on the South Shore of Long Island where I studied accounting, a subject that I hated with a passion. I believe that I was pushed into this course of study to help account for the daily management of the Montauk boys. Part of my job on the Project was to help balance the left and right brain of the computer systems through mentalist activity. In the same way, the debits and credits in accounting taught me how to balance the two halves of a ledger. Each part of my life supported and enhanced activity in the other. Little did I realize at the time how unbalanced my life really was.

An interesting allergy developed during my last year in college. At Christmas break, I was scheduled to have four wisdom teeth and a molar removed. During the

61

surgery, I developed a severe reaction to the anesthesia, sodium pentathol. My heart and breathing stopped. Immediately, the oral surgeon gave me oxygen and used an electric device to shock my heart. The surgery was completed while I was awake but medicated.

Years later, several medical professionals told me that it is extremely unusual to be allergic to sodium pentathol. Only people who have had it used on them extensively develop such severe reactions. Sodium pentathol is also known as "truth serum." Given to spies under interrogation, it is used to make them reveal secret information that they may be concealing. Could this have been one of the chemicals that was injected into me while I was on the table at Montauk Point? I definitely recall the needles, but I have no idea what they contained. Perhaps sodium pentathol can be used for programming the human (or alien) mind.

One of my first major trips overseas also occurred during my college years. It was sponsored by a Zionist organization that sought to bring volunteers to Israel and promote colonization of the arid land there. People from all over the world were recruited, indoctrinated, and sent to various collective farms called kibbutzim. A kibbutz is probably the most pure form of communism that exists in the world. No one receives any more than any other member. A red Soviet flag bearing the hammer and sickle flies over every kibbutz. Even the land is owned by the government; no individual owns anything. The only incentives to produce are loyalty to the homeland, plus your every need is taken care of for you. Consciously, I did not want to go, but I was compelled beyond my own rationalizations and the warnings of my family.

My trip to the Middle East was long and interesting. Travelling by way of France, Italy, and Greece, I found the island of Crete to be exhilarating and the volcano at Stromboli in Sicily to be eye-catching. Although the Pompeii volcano near Naples seemed to open up memories of a prior existence, I was mostly absorbed in what lie ahead of me. During part of the trip, a French woman with Italian citizenship tried to convince me to become a medical doctor and marry her daughter. The entire idea seemed absurd to me at the time, but in retrospect, perhaps I should have taken her up on the offer!

When I landed in Israel, I suddenly became overwhelmed with emotion. As the plane descended into Lod airport over Tel Aviv, tears welled up in my eyes. I felt as if I was finally coming home. I have no explanation for my feelings, yet most of my consciousness was fearful and apprehensive. I fully intended to arrive at the airport; then take the next flight back to the U.S.

At this point, I ask the reader to follow the events slowly and carefully. Although the following passages may become a bit confusing, I am reporting them in the way I recall them. Keep in mind that this series of events confused me, also. However, I have done my best to relate these illogical sequences as logically as possible.

An inexplicably strange thing happened upon my arrival. After leaving the plane, I found myself wandering through the gate areas. In my mind, I wanted to get to the luggage claim area to retrieve my bags so that I could find a flight back. Looking up at a departure board, I saw a flight boarding for Teheran, Iran. I felt as if I should be on it. I stood transfixed at this location until someone asked me to move. Although I thought only a few seconds had passed, I realized when I looked at my watch that almost an hour had passed!

Next, a second event out of the ordinary occurred. While again trying to find the baggage claim area, I stopped in my tracks and was compelled to look up. On another departure board, was a flight to Addis Ababa, Ethiopia; Nairobi, Kenya; and Johannesburg, South Africa. Once more, I was transfixed. I saw myself board this flight with a group of people, then take off knowing that I would return to Israel without anyone realizing that I was gone. Another student on my original flight jolted me awake and said that he had found a way to retrieve our luggage. This guy claimed to be a rabbinical student from Georgia who was here to see the Holy Land and work on a kibbutz. I did not like him because he was arrogant and always had nasty comments. Something told me that he was not telling the complete truth.

After retrieving our luggage, we proceeded to the area where a representative from American Zionist Youth Foundation was to meet us and take us to the designated kibbutz where we would work for the next couple of months. Three women also waited with us.

Hours passed and no one came to take us to our destination. I do not remember what occurred during this time except that I was sitting on my luggage when a dark-skinned Israeli man arrived. He said that instead of going directly to the kibbutz, he was taking us to a place in Jerusalem for the night. Crammed into his little Renault, we headed for the ancient city. I was so exhausted that I did not appreciate the scenery nor the historic sights that we passed as we climbed the mountains of Judea to the Holy City. Along the way, we passed modern apartment buildings beside hovels as well as remnants of destroyed Jordanian tanks and artillery installations. By law, the city of Jerusalem is built out of "Jerusalem stone" from the surrounding mountains. Because of this, the city blends into the countryside. From a distance, you can hardly tell where the city ends and the countryside begins; it is a magnificent sight. Jerusalem means "City of Peace."

Too tired to eat, all I wanted was a hot shower and a comfortable bed. The women accompanying us were dropped off at a youth hostel for women. The driver then took me and the unfriendly rabbinical student to something that reminded me of a prison. Pulling up to a large stone building with iron gates and fortifications, there were no lights on the inside. The driver remarked that this was an old British army barracks. The size of a small castle, there was no one there but us! After unloading our bags, the driver told us to follow him as he unlocked the padlocks on the front gates. Inside, it was dark, musty, dank, and eerie. We waited in the vestibule while he turned on the electricity. We then followed him up a long narrow staircase to a floor that contained bedrooms of sorts. He directed us into a small cell-like room with two iron cots and two hard wooden chairs. A single light bulb hung from a wire in the middle of the ceiling. Next, he showed us down a long, dim hallway to a large bleak shower room that looked like no one had bathed there since World War II. Telling us that he would return in the morning, he mumbled something about going to Tel Aviv for the night and that it was a long trip. He left abruptly.

My companion hardly spoke a word the rest of the night. We took turns showering in the trickling water, before laying down on the hard and uncomfortable cots to sleep. When the single light bulb was turned off, it was pitch black in the freezing cold room. I could feel the thoughts of all the soldiers who had stayed here. I sensed their loneliness and longing for home. In fact, I felt the same. As thoughts of my family in America and the comforts of home filled my head, I decided that I must be crazy for coming here. The sound of dogs barking and playing outside reminded me of familiar noises from home. This made me feel even more lonely. When I heard a muezzin (a Moslem cleric) start his call for night prayers from the minaret of a nearby mosque, I knew that I "was not in Kansas anymore!"

This next experience is non-sequitur. I believe that these events were "squeezed" or "folded" into linear time. Please follow carefully.

Glancing up, I noticed small balls of light appearing on the ceiling. They seemed to swirl around in white and yellow, then turn blue and green. I felt like I was swirling with them. I followed them with my eyes until I simply could not keep them open anymore. Suddenly, I was back at the Tel Aviv airport—it was the day that I arrived and I was boarding a plane for Teheran. I had no luggage except a small carry-on bag that was not mine. The event seemed strange, but somehow I knew what I was doing.

I remember taking off and flying northwest instead of east toward Iran. A man sitting next to me told me in perfect Hebrew that Israeli aircraft cannot fly over Arab territory. Therefore, we were flying northwest into Turkish airspace. Next, we would turn east and continue into Iranian territorial space. This was 1975 and there was no peace treaty in place. In fact, there was talk of another war. As the peaks of the Anatolian mountain range came into view, a voice over the intercom instructed us to pull the window shades down as we crossed into Iranian airspace. Iranian fighter jets would be pacing the plane, and if they observed an unshielded window, there could be trouble. I was told that this was done only with aircraft that did not fly a regular route and might be suspected of spying on Iran or surrounding territories.

I remember the dusty and minaret-filled skyline of Teheran. A few skyscrapers appeared as testimony to the modernization program of the Shah. Next, I remember leaving the aircraft as it stood on the tarmac. Alone, I entered a small, shiny black car. We drove through narrow streets, then onto a major highway that led outside the city into high snow-covered mountains. Turning off of a one-lane road, we travelled on twisted paths. Suddenly, we made a sharp left turn into a black opening on the side of a mountain cliff. As we emerged into the cave, I flashed back to Johannes von Gruber appearing in the underground cavern.

At this point, I ask the reader to understand that most human memories are linear. That is, one event follows another in sequential time order. In my case, my consciousness spans multiple time lines and realities. One alternate universe bleeds through to another, and I am cognizant of this all at once due to my mind being opened through Kundalini activation.* I must learn to focus on a specific event in order to comprehend it. In this chapter, I am attempting to list the events in the order I experienced them. Actually, all the events occurred simultaneously, but the human mind can only decipher one at a time.

The rest of my time in Iran consists of memory flashes. I heard the Hebrew, Farsi (Persian), and German languages spoken along with an occasional flurry of Russian. For the most part, I felt drugged and disoriented. I remember two scientists in white coats entering the room where I sat. They spoke to me in German. I also recall a painful physical examination in the nude. After this, a metallic cap was placed on my head which seemed to send flashes of information shooting into my brain. I know this was programming me to perform some function. My captors then took me far away from "prying eyes" as they

---

* Kundalini activation refers to all chakra centers opening up in sequence, thus allowing the mind to be 100% utilized and aware of many realities simultaneously.

described their reasoning. Taken to an elevator, I was strapped into a seat beside them. The elevator then rushed downward at a tremendous speed. At this point, I briefly flashed back to my trip as a young boy in the small craft with the plant-like alien. The pressure of the high speed caused my skin to flatten against my bones and my teeth to tightly clench together. When the elevator jolted to a halt, I felt ill.

My legs were so heavy that it was difficult to walk. In addition, I realized that I had wet myself. I was placed into an elongated diamond-shaped vehicle that waited at a platform similar to a train station. Both in front and behind it was a tubular tunnel which seemed infinite. As the door closed behind me, I noticed two older men dressed in black suits and white shirts already inside. The vehicle glided along, increased rapidly in speed, then started to hum. One of the men smiled at me, remarking that we were on a hyperspace subway system that circled the globe. "No one knows who built it," he added, "but our alien friends showed us how to use it and build more."

I think that I must have fallen asleep because when I awoke, I was at the airport again; this time boarding a flight to Johannesburg by way of Addis Ababa and Nairobi. The same two older men were with me, apparently supporting me on either side. Even though I thought this was odd, a part of me accepted the predicament and knew what was happening. It was a "deja vu" of my trip to Iran. I was confused, but in my life, the unconventional is the norm.

After taking off and heading south over the Negev desert, the plane followed the Red Sea for some time. On the left of the aircraft was the coastline of Saudi Arabia. On the right was Egypt, then Sudan. My travel companions told me that anti-aircraft guns were on us every step of the way. Any change of course to either coastline would result in enemy fire — a comforting thought while travelling helplessly in the air! I prayed that the pilot had a steady hand on the controls.

As we passed the coastline of Sudan, we made a sharp turn to the west. I straightened up in my seat, trying to speak, but no voice came out. I did not know if it was from fear, dryness, or both. One of my companions stated that we were headed for the coastline of Ethiopia and the mainland of Africa, and this meant that we were safe. I always sat by the window. One escort sat on the aisle and left an empty seat between us. The other one sat on the aisle directly across from us. We landed in Addis Ababa only long enough to refuel and board a few passengers. I did not leave my seat, not even to use the bathroom. Ethiopia looked disgusting and dirty. The air felt dry, making me cough. The surrounding area was a desert.

The short hop to Nairobi took a little over an hour. There seemed to be more grassland and nature preserves here. Nairobi had an impressive skyline for Africa. Even so, the airport was primitive, hot, and without air-conditioning. Here, I was allowed to accompany a companion to a bathroom. The toilets were filthy and the floor was covered in sand and dirt. Lizards hung on the doors and ceiling vents. I felt uncomfortable and out of place. Back on the plane again, we flew over beautiful and lush tropical forests on the way to Johannesburg. I saw a magnificent snow-capped mountain that I was told was Mt. Kilimanjaro. A strange aura surrounds that place. In fact, I would not be at all surprised to find out that there is an underground base of some kind located there.

In a gorgeous mountain range, I saw what looked like a volcano. My escort said we were flying over Zaire. As the green below turned yellow and brown, I was told we were crossing between Zimbabwe (Rhodesia at the time) and South Africa. As we touched down in Johannesburg, he told me to prepare for an exciting experience.

The plane was stopped before reaching the terminal. Soldiers in brown uniforms, who reminded me of pictures I had seen of Nazi soldiers, whisked us off the plane and took us by jeep to a small plane waiting at a grassy area of the runway. Watching the El Al 707 then continue towards the terminal, I told my escort that I was afraid to fly in small planes. That was a mistake because he immediately jabbed me with something sharp in my right bicep. The next thing I remember is waking up strapped into a small seat by a window looking down on farmland. I was told we were going to a very important meeting in Capetown.

I must have dozed off again because, when I awoke, I saw beautiful beaches and a pretty city. As we landed, I fell unconscious again. When I woke up, I was naked and strapped spread-eagle on a hard, cold table in a window-less room with brick walls. I saw soldiers with Nazi-like uniforms, an older man in a dark blue uniform that looked American, and a hideous little grey, mostly white in color, who reminded me of the Gumby cartoon character. Because I was not wearing my glasses, I had to squint really hard to see people.

Feeling pain in my penis and groin, I looked down to see a tube inserted into the tip of my penis. I felt clamps around my testicles. Any movement increased the pain. Although the room was cool, I was sweating profusely. I wanted to cry, but no tears flowed. I wanted to scream, but had no voice. The others in the room became aware of my activity. Speaking in perfect English, the man in the dark blue uniform told me not to be afraid. He said that I was part of a great plan to benefit mankind on many worlds— if I survived. Thanks a lot! I must have passed out again because when I regained consciousness, I was sitting on a bench against a wall. I was naked except for a white towel draped over my waist. Men stood in front of me and called my name in Hebrew. Their voices seemed kind, but I disliked them intensely. I was embarrassed. When they asked me how I felt, I replied with a curt, "Fine."

Standing against the opposite wall behind them was a tall Sirian described earlier in the book. Telepathically, he told me that he was an ambassador to the Israelis and their allies from the planet Khoom in Sirius A. As part of their race, I had a mission to complete. In time, I would understand and forgive them for what they did. Certain cells of my body had been programmed with information for future use. Only specific methods could extract the information at the appropriate time. My body was built for this purpose because I had a unique energetic structure. One day, I would return to Khoom to help my people overcome some of their destructive mind-patterns. My experiences here, as well as in other star systems, was vitally important to this mission.

The next thing I remember, I was on that vehicle in the tube again, traveling underground at high speed on the hyperspace subway. Opening my eyes, I saw my two companions smile at me. At that moment, I hated them, wanting to lash out and kill them; but I could not move even one fiber of my being. I could only look and hate. A moment later, I was awake on that awful cot in the barracks in Jerusalem. Naked, I was exhausted beyond all human comprehension and covered in grimy sweat. The nasty student was already in the shower. My watch said 8:00 A.M. As I dragged myself out of bed, my body felt like it was under tons of concrete. I had to get ready to leave for the kibbutz. What had I just experienced? Was it a hallucination? Did I remember or relive an actual event? My mind said no; my body said yes.

7

AT THE KIBBUTZ

The women were already in a little van when we came outside to load our luggage. We were told that there had been a change of plans. The rich kibbutz up north in Galilee was booked solid, so we were going to a poor kibbutz called Gvar Am, which means the strength, or conquering, of people. This kibbutz was located next to the Gaza Strip in the Negev desert. The nearest Israeli city was Ashkelon. The trip to Gvar Am was horrendous. Israelis do not drive their cars, they aim them. Stopping in Ashkelon, we waited for a kibbutz representative to take us the rest of the way. The downtown area teemed with Palestinian workers who had crossed the border to earn a living. Because they would try to con us out of our possessions, we were told to stay away from that area. The city itself was typical of the Middle East with busy roads, hordes of humanity, and overwhelming smells that quickly dispelled any hunger pangs.

The representative soon arrived, whisking us away to our new home. Housed in the first cottages built by the original settlers from Germany in the early 1930's, these were the oldest buildings on the property. The stone floors were uneven, reminding me of waves upon an ocean. The walls and roof were wood. Inscribed over the porch was a line from an old Hebrew song: "Heenay ma tov u ma nayim shevet achim gom yachad...Behold how good and wonderful for brothers to live together." I wonder if by "brothers" they meant the human-sized roaches or the airplane-sized wasps!

The air was hot and dry; the natives rather unfriendly. I suppose they thought it presumptuous of foreigners to work at this kibbutz for awhile, then return to their wealthy countries to tell tales of building the homeland. In the meantime, they stayed and suffered a miserable existence. It did not take long for the young boys of the settlement to ask for our possessions. Remember, this was a purely communistic society where no one was allowed to have any more than anyone else.

Rising at 4:30 A.M. every day, we reported to the pear groves by 5 A.M. Breakfast was served at 8:00 A.M. but not before some of the Scottish volunteers became exhausted and passed out from the heat. After breakfast, we saluted the red flag, complete with hammer and sickle, then returned to work. By noon, it was too hot to work, so we returned to our quarters for lunch. The afternoon was free, but there was no place to go.

At this kibbutz, I made a friend from England. We enjoyed working together and remained in contact for many years; even visiting each other in our respective countries. Several years later, I learned that he was an agent for both British and Soviet intelligence.

I soon had enough of Spartan communist living and decided to escape from the kibbutz. To officially leave, their council has to vote upon it. I was not taking any chances with their decision; so early one morning, before sunrise, I packed my things to go. Intending to search for relatives in the town of Holon, I found myself in the midst of another adventure that I had not planned to take.

The bus ride to Tel Aviv was long and hot. The air along the coast is humid, not dry like it is inland. Sitting on the bus with my ample luggage beside me, wary passengers eyed me for possible terrorist activities. In those days, as in the present, terrorism on buses was rampant. A foreigner with luggage on a bus was extremely suspicious.

Upon my arrival at the central bus station in Tel Aviv, I found myself thoroughly confused. A thousand buses seemed to be going everywhere in the country. Hordes of people tried to dash about in a sea of humanity. After much physical exertion, I managed to find what I hoped was the bus to Holon. As I paid my fare, I asked the driver, who was an older fatherly type, to kindly let me know where to disembark. We drove for what seemed like hours. Finally, I was the only one left on the bus. When I reminded the driver about my stop, he replied that he had forgotten and would personally drive me in the bus to my exact address. Unfortunately, all I knew was the street and town. He had never heard of the street, so he did his best by taking me to a major thoroughfare. Not exactly the kind of treatment you find in New York City.

He left me on a street corner just before dark. I thanked him as he drove off. Alone, tired, hungry, and scared, I started walking down the old narrow streets, fully aware that I did not have a clue where I was going. I decided to look for a place to sleep in the street. The next day, I would get to the airport and fly home. No place looked safe to sleep, so I continued my aimless walking.

Suddenly, I stopped in front of a very old stone building that could easily have fit into a movie about the Casbah. Although there was no light on in the entry way, I felt drawn inside. Ascending the ancient stairways, I heard families chattering away in Hebrew and Arabic. Distinct Middle Eastern smells floated around me.

Finally, stopping on the fifth floor, I went to a door and knocked. Thinking I would ask for advice or maybe a place to sleep, an old man came to the door. His name was Leon, and he spoke only Hebrew and Polish. When I told him my name, he smiled. He said that he was expecting me!

As the unexpected was the norm in my life, this man turned out to be the husband of my grandmother's cousin. Unseen forces led me directly to his door. He phoned his daughter, and she brought her entire family to meet me. I returned to her home where I stayed for the next two months. They had never met me before, nor did I even know their names. This was truly an unexpected, but welcome, miracle.

8

THE SIRIANS

The apartment in Holon became my home base. From there, I left on many trips around the region, sometimes for days at a time.

One particular adventure took place while on an excursion to the Negev desert in the south of Israel. I had just passed the restricted area around Dimona, a town where Israel has its secret nuclear facility. This place is guarded by the Falasha, the Black Jews from Ethiopia who claim to be descendents of King Solomon and the Queen of Sheba. The Queen supposedly returned to Ethiopia with the original Ark of the Covenant where it remained for safekeeping until only a few years ago.

King Solomon was a powerful mystic. His advisors always discussed the future with him. It is believed that he was warned of a future time when Israel would be overrun with evil foreigners. The Holy Ark of the Covenant would most likely be a prime target.

I believe that Solomon, in all his wisdom, decided to hide the real Ark of the Covenant in a place where no one would think to look. Conveniently, the Queen of Sheba was looking for a major token of faith and affection from her current lover. Solomon sent the Ark back with her to Ethiopia and made a facsimile for the public to view.

In order to solidify his trust for Sheba and the Ark, Solomon saw to it she had his child so that she would always feel an obligation to her child's people. His was the perfect plan.

The Queen's descendents became the Falasha, a numerous faction in Ethiopia. At one time, it is believed that there were over 500,000 Falasha in Ethiopia. In fact, Haile Salassie, the ruler of Ethiopia until a military coup toppled his regime, called himself the "Lion of Judah." The Israeli Mossad, or intelligence agency, helped the province of Eritrea break away from Ethiopia because the Ark was hidden there and the military government refused to cooperate with the Israelis. Consequently, the Israelis created their own country with whom to negotiate. The Ark was successfully transferred to the Holy Land at the same time the military government of Ethiopia allowed the Israelis to airlift all of the remaining Falasha out of Ethiopia. A strange turn of events, but one that portends the coming of the Messiah for the Jews.

It was near Dimona that I was abducted by the Sirians for a major adventure. As I walked around some rock formations that jutted up out of the desert, the sun was hot and the air extremely dry. Perspiration evaporated in a manner of seconds after appearing on my skin. Suddenly, a tremendous flash of light blinded me. Raising my hands to shield my eyes, I realized that there were no sounds around me; in fact, there was an eery silence all about.

Opening my eyes, I found myself in a great room that resembled an ancient Greek or Roman throne room with huge columns and a screen on the wall. Lighting was subdued and without a visible source. There were no windows or doors. From a space near the screen, a tall Sirian dressed in a white and blue robe appeared. He was nearly identical to the Sirian I had seen as a child. About seven-feet tall, his skin was pale. He had large pointed ears, a long pointed nose, and big, blue almond-shaped eyes. His mouth and lips were very small. His fingers appeared long and graceful as he stood in front of me with outstretched arms. The way his robe touched the floor, combined with the shape of his elongated head, he looked exactly like a living ankh! What a beautiful sight! I felt no fear because I had seen one before and felt "at home" with it. The screen came on behind him and allowed me to see the outline of Earth as we moved swiftly away from it in some sort of a craft heading toward Mars. In that room, there was no sensation of movement. It felt soft and comfortable — even more comfortable than home.

The being moved forward and smiled, telepathically welcoming me. Through his thoughts, he told me that we were on our way to Mars to see something that would help me at a later time. Continuing, he said that his species created people from stock brought to Earth from elsewhere. These creations are known as Hebrews, as is their language. Much of this had been distorted and interfered with over the millenniums. His species was now in league with the remnants of these original creations, the Israelis, to correct and purify them before the next wave of interruptions occur. Apparently, the Sirians felt that these Hebrew remnants were not the genetically-whole beings that they originally created. Because it was too late to change their physical structure, it had become necessary to change their mind-patterns, thus enabling them to interface with other alien beings. As he communicated, pictures of his words appeared on the screen behind him. I actually saw history from the dim past as though it was happening at that moment.

Next, I remember lying on a table in a brightly lit clinical-looking room. The Sirian was there with a tall grey being who had round, black eyes and a goofy look on its face. Identified to me as a Vegan, it was a creation by the Sirians out of their own genetics mixed with the little greys. Although not strapped down, I could not move, and I realized that I was naked. For the first time, I felt fear with the Sirians. A bright device was placed over my face as they probed my genitals, stomach, and chest. The Sirian said that they needed to test for residuals of genetic resonance identifying my body with theirs. He said they had manufactured my body in collusion with certain Earth forces for the purpose of completing their agenda. I was some kind of pawn in an interstellar game. What was going on here?

To complicate matters further, he said that my soul-personality was some type of entity from a nonphysical aspect of Sirius which was an even higher form than himself. My body contained Sirian DNA which was necessary for the soul-personality to operate it. As he spoke, I began to glimpse in my mind my true identity which was simultaneously magnificently beautiful and frightening. Tears flowed uncontrollably down my face. This seemed to amuse the Sirian and the Vegan. I thought to myself, "If I looked like either one of you, I would not laugh!"

Next, I was stood up instantaneously. Wearing only a Sirian robe, I could not see my feet. I felt elation, like I was on a natural high. I cannot compare the feeling to anything another can understand without having had the experience themselves. I felt a complete knowing of all things; a connection to all beings. Yet, I retained my identity of self. I followed the Sirian out through the wall to what appeared to be a maroon-colored cave with a high ceiling that seemed to go on for miles. Glancing back, I saw the craft that I had just been in — it resembled a gigantic pearl. Completely white, with a soft whitish-violet glow, there was no sound coming from it. Instantly, I knew that it travelled through space like an electron as it becomes a particle wave — somewhere between the physical and spiritual planes.

In front of me, I saw a large group of men. Most of them were in their twenties, a few were teenagers, and some were older. Digging in unison with shovels, they moved like automatons. Large, melon-headed beings watched them work. Apparently, these were their overseers. A few four-foot tall greys moved about. I saw tunnels and crafts that looked like discs. Suddenly, all the men stopped and looked up toward a platform. Loudly, a voice called out, "The Emissary from Rigel will speak now."

At that moment, a five-foot being with round, black eyes appeared on the platform. His large head was draped with a kind of short curtain around the back of it. Dressed all in black, his clothing appeared to be a uniform. Looking ominous, he carried a rod that looked both metallic and crystalline at the same time. Everyone seemed to understand his mental communication. Explaining that this group of men had completed their service on Earth and the Martian outpost, he told them that they would now be examined for possible transport to Rigel for experimentation. Those not used would be eliminated. The men were then led into the open port of a silver disc. I noticed that their legs were chained together. The entire scene appeared to be orchestrated just for me. I do not know if it was. If so, what would be the purpose? Perhaps the entire incident is an implanted memory.

The next thing I remember, I was back on the Sirian ship. Travelling in hyperspace, I sat in a darkened room on the floor with the Vegan and the Sirian. Soft lighting allowed me to see inside and outside the ship simultaneously. Hyperspace was a beautiful shade of dark blue and violet. The ship appeared to be diamond-shaped as it travelled. The Sirian said that we were going back to our home world, Khoom, which orbited Sirius A in that binary star system. Later, I could decide if I wanted to return to Earth. I realized we three were the only beings aboard that great ship. Operated totally by our will, I felt completely safe and at peace. I knew that I was going home.

I do not remember much of my stay on Khoom. I was told that my memory would return at the appropriate time. A frozen world covered in ice and snow, the sun's glare on the surface was blinding. The inhabitants lived underground. An elaborate and impenetrable defense system protected the entire planet. Once a subtropical world, Khoom was pushed out of its original orbit by war eons ago. From space, it looks blue and white. The planet has no moons. A victim of the original battle between good and evil, Khoom was blown from its cradle orbit by those who created the Draco race, the reptilians who seek to dominate the galaxy and beyond. The creators of the Draco races came from another time and space. The first genesis of Lucifer, their name denotes the epitome of evil.

Occupying the same physical location as Khoom, but at a different vibratory resonance, is a nonphysical world governed by a council of nine beings known as the Ohalu Council. While not the same beings referred to as "The Nine" in other literature, they do communicate with The Nine as well as participate in joint projects. "The Nine" first appeared in literature in the works of Dr. Adreja Puharich. In his work with channelers, he came across a few individuals who claimed to be in contact with this ET group. Uri Geller was the first to actually identify them as former physical beings who transferred their minds and soul-essences into nine advanced computers. Each one of these computer represents a different aspect of the Mind of God. "The Nine" communicate with a few select individuals across the planet in an effort to upgrade the collective consciousness of humankind.

The Ohalu Council also governs the planet Khoom in the star system Sirius since the Sirians are really the lower vibrations of the council beings in the same way that humans are lower vibrations of their ET selves.

I was originally sent to Earth by the Ohalu Council who directed the Sirians on the creation of my physical body. They told me there are nine beings on Earth who are like me. Each one is directed by a member of the council. I was shown my past and future while I was on Khoom. I was taken to a planet orbiting Sirius B that was a tropical, swampy jungle world occupied by short, stocky beings who live in huts. Extremely advanced, these creatures can astral project anywhere they want to at will. They rely on others for physical transportation off-world but as they have no need to go anywhere else, they rarely do so. Communicating exclusively by mind-linking, they do not have a spoken language.

The Sirians told me of the coming Earth invasion by the Draco; that the Orion Confederation was working with the Draco; and that there is a war going on right now between the Sirians and Orions. The supreme merchants of the universe, the Sirians actually supplied the Orion groups with the weapons that are now being used against them. However, the Sirians keep the best and most powerful for themselves, so they never lose. The Sirians see the Orions as bad children who play with matches. They do not seek to destroy them, but they keep them in check. They allow humans, Orions, and the Draco to follow their own destinies.

Despite not wanting to leave, the Ohalu Council convinced me to return to Earth. Arriving back in Israel, I found that only three days had passed. I was unceasingly thirsty, had lost ten pounds, and was so tired that I could not see straight. Returning to Holon, I slept for almost an entire week.

During my return "rest," I "realized" that the Ark of the Covenant is actually a communication device between the physical world and hyperspace. The Sirians apparently gave the Hebrews instructions for building it. A reconstruction of the device was built by the University of Minnesota years ago, following the instructions given in the Bible. It was so electrically charged and dangerous that it had to be destroyed.

I believe that the Sirians are trying to undermine the plans of all the factions involved on Earth: the New World Order, the Draco, the Greys, the Tall Blonds, etc. Their agenda is to bring all events to a climax, then usurp all power, possibly via the Israelis. This is only speculation on my part. Time will tell.

9

TWIN FLAMES

I returned to the U.S. to resume my college studies. The nightly faces in the window and various grey abductions continued with renewed vigor. My desire for children and a life companion became an obsession. Then one night, I was taken to a place where I met the most beautiful girl I had ever seen. At the time, I was unaware that she was only sixteen. I had seen her once before at a meeting we boys had with our controllers. We were told that those of us involved with genetic experimentation were to be mated with specific females to produce a particular type of offspring. This project was called "The Marriage Project" or "The First Wife Project."

I was matched with a fourteen-year old girl from Massachusetts whose energetic structure indicated that she was part of my own frequency, known as a "twin soul" in current metaphysical literature. Her name was Mia, which was apropos, since she really was mine. Mock marriage ceremonies were performed which were taken very seriously. Certificates were issued indicating that each couple was officially in union for the express purpose of mating. That evening, those of us who were wed were given a table in a white room where we consummated our marriage. For Mia, the experience was quite uncomfortable. Not only was she a virgin, but many people watched us from behind a glass panel.

For the next two years, Mia and I had no physical contact. Even so, she was constantly in my thoughts and dreams. I knew that we would soon be reunited, hopefully for good. I spent much time and effort looking for a woman who resembled Mia, but to no avail. She had captured my heart and soul. On many occasions, when I travelled at night in hyperspace, Mia was there. White and glowing, she had the energy field of an angel. I only had to think of her to be healed of any ailment. I suspect that she had similar experiences to mine at that time, but she was young and probably did not understand or accept what was happening.

One evening, when Mia was sixteen and I was twenty-four, we were brought together in a clinical environment under the watchful eyes of scientists. Here it was explained that our genetics were perfectly aligned with sequences that were reciprocal to one another. Mia had more Pleiadian genetics; mine were more Sirian. This combination would produce a child of unusual abilities. Brought naked into a white room, we made love three times in succession. The entire episode was dreamlike and almost a blur. At the end, I knew inside of myself that Mia was pregnant. Lying there on the table, she appeared dazed and listless. Subsequently, I was taken away for an extensive examination. I imagine they did the same to her.

One year later, I was informed that I had a child named Jaime. When she was a few months old, I was allowed to see her. I was told that I could have no part in her upbringing in order to avoid contamination of her mind-patterns. She would be closely watched and monitored as she grew up. When she was two-years old, I saw her again. After that, I did not see her for almost twelve years. In my mind, I focused on her to see her thoughts, but it pained me deeply that I had no part in her life. I know that Mia and Jaime had many hardships during those years. I wish that I had been allowed to help them.

Although I desperately longed for a child, I knew that they would always be taken away from me. I was not considered to be the kind of father conducive to bringing up a specially created child because I would be too controlling and domineering. In addition, they were afraid I would teach the child my ways and beliefs, thus preventing the natural flow of information to my own creations.

Mia had a difficult life with her family, eventually ceasing communication with them. Interestingly enough, one of her childhood neighbors became a focal point in my life years later. I will write more about that in a subsequent chapter in this book.

Indeed, Mia and I were and are twin flames. Our soul-personalities were once one. We split off from each other aeons ago when we sojourned on Arcturus. She agreed to a life in the Pleiades, while I continued on to Sirius. Eventually, we both arrived on Earth but never in the flesh at the same time. This was the first instance. When twin flames incarnate at the same time, it means one of two things: either they have a tremendously important mission to complete for their civilization, or the end times are at hand. In our case, it is both. Our pre-Earth history was told to me during a deprogramming session in the early '90's. My memory of her soul-personality has always been strong, even before I knew her in this life line.

Jaime has an extremely awesome potential. She has the ability to see into the future and all possible alternate realities, thus determining the most advantageous path to follow. Imagine what a find this could be for those in power. I spend a lot of time helping Jaime in hyperspace and healing her of any disturbances. Currently involved in her teenage life, she does not realize her potentials. I wrote a book exclusively to Jaime, but so far, she will not read it. Her mother keeps it until Jaime is ready to learn her truth. I do not want to see her make the same mistakes that her mother and I made. She will always be protected; powers much higher than the government and I keep watch over her.

In recent years, Mia and I became reacquainted. We are both healing old and current wounds. Mia has come to me for counseling and for aid in remembering our past experiences. I will always be here for her.

Currently, Mia is experiencing a difficult period. This is part of the purging of negativity from her mind-patterns. She must choose a path — either the light way or the dark side. If she chooses correctly, her abilities will increase.

Jaime is also being difficult and stubborn and, in many ways, reminds me of myself. Although she is not pursuing a close relationship with me now, the time is soon approaching when she will need me to train her for her life's adventure.

10

MARRIAGE

When I graduated from college, a family friend found a job for me in New York City. Amazingly, the symbol of the company, Sterling Drug, Inc., was the ankh! I detested the daily 100 mile round-trip commute. Additionally, I got up extremely early in the morning to prepare myself for the long day ahead. Part of my programming compelled me to exercise at least one hour in the morning and another hour when I returned home. My morning exercise routine consisted of weight-lifting and isometrics. The evening one was almost completely aerobic with some weight-training thrown in. I did not eat breakfast or lunch unless my mother prepared them for me. During my lunch hour, I walked rapidly around the crowded streets for a minimum of three miles. In the summer, I was drenched with sweat by the time I returned to the air-conditioned skyscraper on Park Avenue. In the winter, I walked in the snow, ice, and freezing temperatures. I simply had to move and exercise. I could not control it; it controlled me. I did not have an ounce of fat on my body, but even so, everyone thought that I was crazy.

During this time, my nightmares worsened. The dream about trying to escape from an underground facility kept recurring. I was always caught and always woke up screaming. I also kept seeing Mia in the night. Taken to a greyish-silver room, I was shown a pregnant Mia with a picture of the fetus on the wall behind her. Little did I know then that this was a sonogram.

The worst of the experiences was being strapped down naked to a metallic table and hooked up to some kind of machinery. At one point, I saw the inside of my body on a wall screen as they performed surgery on me. You may ask who "they" were. I really do not know for sure. Sometimes I saw alien-looking beings of different species. Many times, I saw human beings wearing white medical coats.

Once, I was strapped to a wall with my nipples and genitalia connected to wires and a device that glowed violet and green. After awhile, I was taken down and wrapped in a white sheet that reminded me of a toga. Brought to an austere, drab, and dimly lit room, there was only a small wooden table and a chair for me to sit upon. A woman and man soon entered wearing what appeared to be medical uniforms. The male doctor sat on the table next to me while the redheaded female stood in front of me holding a clipboard. She spoke to me in Russian; the man spoke to me in German. I answered each in their own language. They asked how I was and told me the results of the tests that they did.

They both left the room for a few moments while I sat alone and waited. Even though I was extremely tired, I understood perfectly why I was there and what I had to do. I remember thinking that I had to go to work the next morning and wanting to go back to bed. A clock on the wall read 2:00 A.M.

When the two of them came back into the room, I was embarrassed to talk about the sexual information that the woman asked of me. She was older, about fifty, and I thought that if she were a man, it would be easier to answer her questions. I looked at the man whenever she spoke to me. They both said that the experiments would be repeated in the future using similar types of donors. When I asked what they were talking about, they referred to the child that I had with Mia. Next, they told me that my marriage to Mia was over, to go out in the world for awhile, and develop a conventional life if possible. Confused, I said that I wanted to see my child. The next thing I remember is the alarm going off in my bedroom and realizing that I had to get up for work. Exhausted, I was naked and all of the covers were on the floor. Feeling as if I had a hangover, I put on my robe and went to the bathroom. My penis was red and it burned when I urinated. My back hurt and my neck was stiff. I could not get those two doctors out of my head all day. Even now, they still haunt my thoughts.

At the time, I was employed by a pharmaceutical manufacturer as an internal auditor. This position required extensive travel for weeks at a time and did not allow me to have much of a social life.

I met Michele, my first wife, when I asked for and received a transfer to a division which was permanently based in New York. She worked as a secretary for one of the research doctors in the company. Another secretary introduced us thinking that it would be great if it worked out because we both lived on Long Island. I really did not care for Michele because she was nasty and opinionated, but something made me ask her out over a holiday weekend. So sure that we were not going to hit it off, I arranged two other dates. I saved Michele for last since it would just be a one time date.

We went out to lunch and took a walking tour of Port Jefferson, my favorite town on Long Island. We visited all the quaint tourist shops, watched the ferry as it left for

Bridgeport, then talked about our future plans and goals. Surprisingly, we had similar ideas. We both wanted to get married, have children, take leisurely vacations, and basically lead conventional lives.

By the time I took her home that evening, I knew a lot about Michele and her family. There were things that I did not like, but we did have many things in common. I was afraid to tell her about my secret life in these experiments. I knew it would chase away even the most brave-hearted of women.

I continued to see Michele even though my heart told me that it was wrong. There was simply something about her that annoyed me. Perhaps it was her temper, or perhaps it was the way she spoke to people. It may even have been her dysfunctional family. I should have heeded my own feelings, but once again, I was driven by an order within my mind that I could not control. Michele was not my ideal. I pined for Mia, but in the end, we married.

Our engagement took everyone by surprise, including me! I had only known her for a month. In fact, I did not ever ask her to marry me. One afternoon, as we sat in her car by the docks in Babylon, everything suddenly became still. Stopping our rather ordinary conversation, we stared at each other for what seemed like an eternity. Then, just as suddenly, everything returned to normal as we noticed movement again outside. Taking deep breaths at the same time, we agreed to rush home to tell everyone about our impending marriage. I did not want to do this; neither did she. I guess we'll never really know what happened, but it was a done deal.

When I told my parents, they were unimpressed. She had the same reaction from her parents. I bought her a ring, making it public at my father's 50th birthday party. The night before his party, we made love without any protection. This resulted in her first pregnancy. We decided, or rather she decided and I acquiesced, that she would have an abortion. She did not want to look pregnant when she walked down the aisle.

In retrospect, I am sorry that I did not try to stop her. I now believe that abortion is wrong unless the mother's life is in danger or the pregnancy is a result of rape. I also understand that the soul-personality does not enter into the body until the first breath, but it is that soul-personality, and no one else, that must decide whether or not to continue the life-stream. People who do not want children should take the proper precautions before the pregnancy, not destroy a possible life-stream after it is created. Although that may sound fundamentalist to some, it is what I know to be the proper way.

Our engagement should have been a warning about our future marriage. There were fights and disagreements. At one point, she wanted to call it off because she was not in love with me. Well, I was not in love with her either, but for some reason that I could not understand, I had to be married now. There was not any time to look for someone else! I talked her into going forward with the plans.

After going to bed one evening, I received a mental visit from a being that I can only describe as an energy pulse. It had no form, yet it was familiar to me. Although it had no gender, it seemed more masculine than feminine. Appearing to sense my distress at my choice for a marriage partner, it literally comforted me with waves of light energy. Speaking telepathically, it said that all was as it was supposed to be. This woman had agreed to be the vessel for the entry of my children into the physical plane. The marriage would not be a permanent situation. Apparently, I had agreed to this as part of the experiment. I was lucky not to have the same destiny as most of the others involved in the Montauk Project. Most of them would never know the feelings of parenthood or even have relationships in the outside world. One day, it continued, I would know the truth about myself, but until then, I was at the mercy of those who controlled my life.

After that experience, I acted with a renewed determination and felt as if I was on a mission that had to be completed. Our beautiful and expensive wedding was followed by a wonderful honeymoon in Acapulco. Upon returning, we rented a spacious apartment in Bayside, Queens. From the back windows, we could see the Manhattan skyline. With wonderful jobs, we seemed to be on an upward spiral, but only God and my watchers knew what lay ahead. I wish I had known!

11

STRANGE PHENOMENA

One year after we married, we bought a lot on the South Shore of Long Island near Patchogue. We planned to build a house upon it. Two months after that, Michele unexpectedly became pregnant. Our original plans for the mortgage repayment included both of us working full-time. This was at a time when mortgage rates were near twenty percent.

The financial picture at first looked grim. To our amazement, the builder took three percentage points off the mortgage as a buy down deal. To move one of the last houses in his development, he also threw in many extras. Incredibly, both Michele and I received promotions with raises. This enabled us to pay our monthly debt more easily. Next, Michele received an extended maternity leave with full pay. Despite the odds against us, the "powers that be" put everything into place to get us into that house. As it turned out, Michele needed a Caesarean-section resulting in several extra weeks of disability pay. Although we loved that house, it provided events and occurrences that were more than we bargained for.

Our ranch-style house was located right over one of the tubes of the hyperspace subway that once travelled from the North American continent mainland out onto

Long Island and ended at Montauk Point. From our home, Montauk Point was only a ninety minute drive by car. On several occasions, we saw strange lights over our house traveling out either toward the ocean or the Point.

Exactly one month after we moved in, Michele's parents came from New Mexico. They would stay until the birth of the baby. One freezing cold night in January, we were all at my parents' home for dinner. Michele and I both felt uncomfortable the entire time. As soon as we returned home, we knew something was wrong. The lights we left on were now off and the house had an eerie darkness to it. Upon entering, we found the back glass door smashed to minute pieces. A small TV and costume jewelry were missing. Nothing else was taken and that included my father-in-law's gun and money!

Two plain clothes detectives arrived from the police department to dust for fingerprints, but they found nothing. Outside, the ground was too frozen to provide footprints. When the detectives left, they said that it was probably neighborhood kids looking for drug money. That was hard to believe. The next day, we found the word "Hello" etched into the unbroken side of the smashed glass door. Whoever it was knew exactly what they were doing. It seemed they wanted to let us know that they were around. Nothing of real value was taken and other than the glass door, nothing was damaged, but it was enough to put us on edge.

After my son Matthew was born, my in-laws returned home. Life during the day was normal enough, but the night was another story. We heard strange noises in and around the house, including the sound of footsteps on the roof. At first, we attributed it to the settling of the new house. We then realized that the footsteps always began near the garage on the far end of the house, walked up to our bedroom, stopped, then turned around and went the other way! We thought that it was an animal, but after a particularly heavy snowfall, the noises continued. No animal could have legs long enough to touch the roof through all the deep snow and ice.

On several occasions, a horrific pounding on the ceiling, strong enough to sway the ceiling fan and move the bed, jolted us out of a deep sleep. The third time this happened, I ran outside to observe the bedroom roof. There was nothing there. The sky was clear and the wind was still. This unnerved us even more. What could be doing this?

Another time, shortly after retiring for the night, I heard my house keys jiggle. As I kept them in the kitchen, they were not close by. I felt my blood run cold, but I could not move to check it out. My body simply would not move. The next thing I recall was waking up in the morning after having an abduction dream.

The alien presence in my nightmares and dreams continued with renewed fervor. Almost two or three times each week, I was subjected to visitations in my bed with my eyes wide open. Every time I tried to scream, nothing came out. Whenever I tried to shake Michele awake, she was dead to the world.

Another night, just after we went to sleep, we heard a tremendous crash from the kitchen. Certain that the burglars had returned, I told Michele to call the police while I investigated. In the kitchen, I found the garbage knocked over. All the doors and windows were locked. When the police arrived, they searched outside with flashlights. They said they found nothing strange except our children's little footprints in the mud. I replied that we only had a tiny baby, and he certainly was not running around outside. Following the officers outside, I saw tiny footprints that looked like they were from a child under the age of ten. They began under our bedroom window and continued around the perimeter of the house. Shortly thereafter, we installed an alarm system and built a six-foot high stockade fence all around our property.

One evening, Michele was gone and the baby slept. I sat watching television in the den when a flash of movement from the kitchen caught my eye. Glancing up, I saw a reflection move quickly past the oven door. Thinking it was a reflection from a car passing on the road outside, I realized that the oven faced away from the road, plus all the curtains were drawn shut. About an hour later, I saw the movement again. Then I heard one of the kitchen chairs crash on the floor. I nearly jumped out of my skin!

Slowly, I crept toward the kitchen. All of the lights were on. One of the dinette chairs was moved away from the table but stood upright. These were heavy metal chairs on rollers that we always kept close to the table when not in use. This made me quite nervous, and when my wife came home, I told her what had happened.

She confided that ever since Matthew was born, she felt like she was being watched; especially when she was in the den. Whenever she looked up, she saw a short, caped figure peering at her from behind the corner where the den met the kitchen. As soon as she saw it, it fled rapidly down the hallway toward the bedrooms. This occurred day or night. What was this little figure and why was it watching us? Apparently, it did not mean any harm, but it was either very clumsy or trying to scare us. Definitely a humanoid shape, it only wanted to be seen long enough to let us know that it was there.

Again, my night terrors increased with renewed fervor. Going to sleep became a fearful, anxious experience. At least twice each week, I woke up somewhere else.

Sometimes it was in an alien presence; at other times, I was in a laboratory surrounded by equipment with doctors and scientists working on panels. Invariably, I was naked, lying on a table or platform with probes and wires attached to me.

I once woke up in a long, black tube that was extremely cold. Through windows on the side of the tube, I saw greys working on equipment. I was held down to a cold, metallic table. Wires and pointed objects came out of the side of the tube and touched my body. When I screamed that I was cold and that the instruments hurt me, one of the greys turned to look at me through the window. He mentally replied that it did not matter because I would not remember it anyway. This callous being continued sending probes into my body. One wire-like protrusion entered my penis, and I felt it moving deep inside my body until it reached my testicles. Trying to scream again, I realized that I had no voice. Waking up in my bed, shivering and nauseous, I felt like I had to urinate urgently. When I saw a white pus come out of me, my knees practically buckled from fright.

Another time, I awoke in the middle of the night to a strange glow in my bedroom. Turning to look up, I saw two heads without bodies floating above my bed in midair. Neither human nor alien, they were almost robotic. Talking to each other in a strange language, they actually turned to face each other as they spoke. Occasionally, they glanced down on me. Starting to yell, I had no voice. I tried to wake my wife, but I could not move. Finally, the two heads faded away, returning the room to darkness. At that instant, my voice came back. I bellowed for help and woke my wife. She was by now accustomed to my nightmares.

Several times, my wife dreamed that she was abducted by humans who put her on a table and examined her in front of an Oriental-looking audience. Each time, they checked for a pregnancy. Whenever she had this dream, she soon discovered that she was pregnant.

Once, we both woke up with the same dream to tell each other. We had been chased by tall, blond medical people with strange faces. Placed on a bed for examination, we both got up and tried to run outside but were caught and brought back to the examination room. They told me that I was implanted with a device to increase my sperm count for breeding purposes. I do have a subcutaneous bump in my scrotum that suddenly appeared when I was a teenager in the '70's. I was also told by a medical person at the Montauk base that I was not only a power generator for the mentalists but also used especially for breeding purposes. The aliens were absolutely thrilled with my sperm count.

One night, I heard a noise in the hallway as I fell asleep. A moment later, a parade of short, fat blue people came into my room followed by a grey who appeared to be their leader. Paralyzed, I could not move or speak; my eyes were wide open with fear. I felt them hoist me up above their heads and carry me like a wooden plank. As I watched my bedroom ceiling pass by, it suddenly changed from white plaster to a golden-bronze metallic texture with inlaid designs. Literally propped up onto my feet, I felt my body return to normal. There seemed to be a benevolent air about this experience, the first and only time that ever happened.

I was led through a door that opened like a spiral from a central point and expanded outward into a round room with a circular depression in the middle. Around the depression there was a railing upon which sat a little, blond-haired girl who faced away from me. I saw control panels around the circular walls where some greys sat watching. Two men in military uniforms stepped up to either side of me. They told me to go to the girl because she was waiting for me. A small grey took my right arm and led me to her. As I approached, I saw that her head was rather large for her little body. Her arms were very thin. She wore a sleeveless dress that might be worn by any six or seven-year old. Putting her right arm around my neck, she hugged me to her. Immediately, I felt an overwhelming sensation of love and peace. I wanted to stay with this little girl forever.

One of the military men said that she was my daughter, but she was not human. She was being sent somewhere far away and wanted to see me one more time since she may never see me again. The grey then pulled her arm off of me, and she finally turned to look at me. Her eyes were large ovals, the bluest blue that I had ever seen. Her nostrils were small slits, and she had the very thinnest of lips. She looked so scared and sad that I wanted to cry. Instead, I blacked out. I awoke once more in my bed with a warm, but sad feeling. I felt like I had truly known love.

My house became famous for attacks by the black helicopters that usually fly east towards Montauk Point. In the middle of the night, they hovered only a few feet over the roof and caused my alarms to go off. The batteries ran out quickly. During these "copter attacks" the phone would ring and go dead or there would be a humming sound on the line. Radio stations mysteriously changed and objects disappeared for days before finally returning in odd places.

Despite all of this, coupled with the financial strains, I loved that house and was determined to stay there. My obsession with exercise and physical development grew since my body had to be healthy for the experiments. Ironically, my night fears drove me to drink excessively and even smoke an occasional cigarette. Whenever I drank or smoked, the aliens stayed away, but the humans worked around it.

My life was one big ball of confusion. I was trying to find answers and a path to God; however, whenever I thought I was on the right track, I had another experience which threw me back into the confusion. Feeling as if my mind was not my own, I was unhappy and easily depressed. I was not satisfied with the direction my life was taking.

12

MY CHILDREN

My wife and I had three beautiful baby boys while we lived in our house in Patchogue. All of them were delivered by Caesarean-section. Between pregnancies, Michele developed large and painful ovarian cysts that required surgery to remove them. Her doctor recommended pregnancy to give the ovaries a rest.

Shortly after we moved into the new house in 1983, Matthew was born exactly on his due date. My wife had a dysfunctional labor; so after twelve hours of non-progressive contractions, the baby was delivered by Caesarean-section. Because we had taken natural childbirth classes, this was a great disappointment to us. Weighing over nine pounds, Matthew had rosy cheeks and big, blue eyes with a shock of nearly black hair.

Matthew was a colicky baby. For eighteen months, he screamed every night and refused to sleep. I was the only one who could rock him to sleep. During this time, my wife and I had disturbing dreams about Matthew being taken by strangers. For a long time, we said nothing about our dreams to each other. I continued to have my own usual nightmares of abduction and experimentation. Now, my wife was also being disturbed in her sleep. She thought that I was contagious! We both dreamed that people we did not know took Matthew, later telling us that he was dead. I remember crying hysterically in my sleep before waking up and running into the baby's room to make sure that the dream was not real. Sometimes I heard my wife get up to go into the baby's room. She always commented that she was just checking on him.

One morning while watching the baby play, we discussed leaving him with a baby-sitter. I told her that I was afraid to leave him with a stranger. Starting to cry, she said that she felt the same way and blurted out her dreams. Feeling as if ice water was running through my veins, I shared my identical dreams. We agreed never to leave him alone with anyone other than close family.

During one of my night excursions, I was told that my children were really not mine. As experiments, they are not under my jurisdiction. I must surrender them whenever it was deemed necessary. Determined not to let that happen, this was completely unacceptable to me. At that moment, I swore that I would never give up another child. All of the experimenters would have to kill me first. Little did I realize that this was not a problem for them!

Jeremy was born twenty-five months later. Daniel came along two and one-half years after that. I loved them all more than my own life. I refused to think that any of them might ever experience the same physical and mental torture that I had gone through. Determined to teach them and myself how to prevent this, I saw as time went on that it was a losing battle.

Matthew was an intelligent child. He walked at eight and one-half months and spoke shortly thereafter. His eyes turned dark, looking all too alien. When he was four-years old, he told me about a tall man with glowing red eyes. The man wore black clothing, lived under the ground, and came into his room at night. Knowing that I had never discussed any of my experiences with the children, there was no way Matthew could have learned anything like this from me. Additionally, I closely monitored the television and did not permit him to watch any scary programs.

As he became older, I noticed that whenever a television program involved aliens in any form, he ran from the room. He disliked grey aliens in particular. Always covering his eyes and ears with a pillow, he would beg me to tell him when it was over but would never discuss the subject.

One summer afternoon, after the boys finished riding their bikes in the backyard, we sat under a tree to rest in the shade. Matthew remarked about the blueness of the sky; then pointed to where a large, singular cloud drifted over us. The only cloud in the sky, an eerie feeling compelled us to stare at it. Suddenly, as if it was rapidly erased from one end to the other, the cloud disappeared within a few seconds. It appeared to be peeled out of the sky. When it was completely gone, the boys ran into the house and remained there for the rest of that sunny afternoon.

A couple of months later, I was raking leaves in the backyard. Matthew, who was seven at the time, asked if he could help. After talking about school and other ordinary subjects, Matthew suddenly asked if I knew about the Earth underground. When I told him about the geology of the Earth, he insisted that the Earth had cities inside. He told me that the tall "man in black" came to him at night to teach him about the underground. This man said that he came from the underground and that Matthew was one of them. The man had been sent to the surface to watch my wife and I so that we would not do anything wrong. Was this the same being that Michele and I had seen from the den since Matthew's birth? My child proceeded to tell me how energy was transferred all over the underground by way of energy posts that beamed waves to each other, thus creating a relay system. His description was so intricate that I soon realized this could not come from a seven-year old boy!

Next, Matthew related how the "man in black" hummed in a low pitch that translated into words inside of his head. This being told Matthew that there were humans who lived under Long Island as well as all over the world. Once, they lived on the surface, but now they hid.

As the years passed, Matthew confided more about his nocturnal visitations. A couple of times each week, he was taken out of his body in a vortex. First, he saw his body sleeping on the top bunk bed. Next, he felt himself float through the roof into space where he was attracted to a bright light. After going through this light, he was in a place where grey aliens watched him. Besides giving him things to play with, they also showed him various technologies including the energy pack that powers their ships. Shaped like a football, he held it in his hands. They also showed him weapons that looked like portable rocket launchers and told him that one day he would use these in a battle for Earth. They also told him that when he was older, he would experiment with combining the genetic materials of different species to create better ones. Ever since that time, Matthew has been fascinated with space battles and powerful laser weapons. He even saw himself wounded in a battle with aliens while defending a specific area of this planet. Matthew also sees auras and archetypes around people. He can zoom into a person's frequency and read their mind-patterns, just like I do.

Jeremy, my second son, is a brilliant child who is in an advanced program at school. He has no interest whatsoever in aliens or psychic phenomena. The only time he ever mentioned anything strange was when he was two-years old. I left the book *Communion*, which has a drawing of a grey alien face on the cover, out on the coffee table. Strolling into the room, Jeremy commented that the picture was of a bad man. This was the same man who came into his room at night, took his toys, and never returned them. Indeed, we often missed toys from his room, but we assumed that they were simply misplaced. In fact, all through the 1980's, items frequently disappeared into thin air only to reappear weeks or months later. Usually they were gone for good, but whenever they did show up, it was always in a strange place such as the freezer, the far back corner of a closet, or behind the oven.

My youngest son at that time, Daniel, entered into this world in an interesting way. When my wife was four months pregnant, a blood test revealed an odd protein level indicating a possibility of Down's Syndrome or spina bifida. Needless to say, we were upset until we received the results of the amniocentesis indicating a normal male child. However, shortly before the doctor called with these results, I had a terrifying abduction experience.

Taken from my bed in the middle of the night by the four-foot greys, I screamed but could not wake my wife. I was taken to a ship and into a narrow, brightly lit silver-white room without furniture. A female grey came into the room holding a small bundle. No one told me that she was female. I simply knew that "it" was a she. As she approached, a male voice said that she wanted to show me something. Slowly unwrapping the top of the blanket, the female revealed an adorable blond-haired baby. The male voice said that it was mine, and asked if I wanted to hold it. Replying that I did, the female started to unwrap the whole baby, revealing an octopus-like torso with legs instead of a human body. Screaming and crying at the same time, I told them to take it away. The same voice said that it was going to an aquatic world and that I would never see it again. Waking up in my bed, I prayed with all my might that Danny would be a normal child. I cannot describe my relief when the doctor called with the positive test results.

When Danny started to talk, he told me about a man with a clown face who came into his room at night to take him flying. He said that when the man put a magic wand in the middle of his forehead, they immediately were in a place that had balloon lights of different colors.

Once Danny woke up with scratches all over his face. When I asked him why he scratched himself like that, he replied that the clown man took him to meet his baby sister. Reaching out to touch her face, she scratched him with her nails because she had claws instead of fingers! One scratch on the bridge of his nose left a scar that remains to this day. In fact, Danny has a scar showing stitches on his chest even though he has never had surgery in that area of his body.

Danny has the ability to see and communicate with Angels. He asks them questions about the future, and they answer with amazing accuracy. These are not alien beings but angelic entities who come to him at night while he is wide awake. They do not take him anywhere nor do they touch or frighten him.

13

CIA RECRUIT

During the years in Patchogue, we took a number of family trips to Montauk Point. Oddly, I always looked forward to going, but upon arriving, I felt a sensation of dread and foreboding. Then, I wanted to go home immediately. This disturbed the rest of the family who wanted to stay and explore after driving for an hour and a half.

I had nightmares both before and after every trip to Montauk. My thoughts constantly reverted to the night in 1976 when a UFO followed us home after eating dinner in the town of Montauk. Physically, I felt a cold shudder from the base of my spine to the top of my head. Next, my hair became full of static. Goose bumps covered my body accompanied by a constant urge to urinate and coldness in my stomach. I felt as if a mild electrical shock had run through my entire body.

Strangely, after visiting Montauk, I always received Hebrew letters in my brain. They either flashed in front of my eyes or simply appeared in my thoughts. Sometimes, I woke up from a deep sleep and remembered information about the sequences of the letters. I became fascinated with pyramids and their relationships to Egypt and Atlantis. I even knew that a remnant of Atlantis was located on Long Island.

Somehow, I felt that I needed to get away from the entire situation. My marriage was not good. We fought constantly and were verbally abusive in front of the children. I hated my job and I started to hate who I was: a man with an obscure past, unable to tell anyone about it, and a future of abductions, nightmares, and obsessions. Not a pretty picture.

For these reasons, I religiously read the "Help Wanted" section of the Sunday newspaper hoping to find a path out of my messy situation. One day, a little ad in the corner of the paper popped out, imbedding itself so deeply in my mind that I had to respond. The ad said that the CIA was looking for both domestic and overseas agents, to hand-write a letter of application, and send it to an address in Maryland. I scribbled something in pencil on a piece of white paper and mailed it. My wife thought that I was crazy, but then again, she always did.

I had never seen an ad like this before nor have I seen one like it since. Because it was such a strange ad, I mentioned it to several people whom I knew read the want ads with the same fervor that I did. No one had seen the ad! I started to think that I was insane again.

Weeks went by without a word. One night, at 2:00 A.M., the phone rang. I heard my wife say, "Do you realize what time it is?" Then, she abruptly handed me the phone saying, "It's for you — your friends in Washington!"

A man's voice told me that they received my letter and repeated that he was my friend in Washington. Did I understand? "Yes," I replied. Continuing, he said that soon I would receive a large package in the mail containing important psychological testing for both myself and my wife. When we completed the paperwork within the specified time period, I was to mail it back and wait for further instructions.

Per our conversation, a special delivery envelope arrived containing two extremely large testing booklets for Michele and I. Also included were forms for personal information regarding relatives, recent and childhood friends, reactions to various circumstances, and likes and dislikes. Lastly, the envelope contained a form for a complete physical exam. This included an extensive blood test to be filled out by a medical doctor. We were given ten days to either complete all of this or return everything. Rushing about like a madman, I managed to get all of the information and complete the required tests. Several times during these nights, I received phone calls asking if I had any questions. Each call was made by a different person who gave names that I knew were fictitious.

I soon received a confidential letter giving me a fictitious name to use whenever I contacted them: Nathan Diton. My instructions were to completely destroy the letter and never to reveal this name, not even to my wife. Then, I was given a safe phone number, told to go to a pay phone during specific hours, and call them using this name. My call would then be routed to the appropriate person.

The next late night call directed me to the Hyatt Regency Hotel in New York City. I was instructed to report on a specific day and at a specific time to call my contact in a hotel room from the courtesy phone in the lobby. After giving my fictitious name, I had to wait for my call to be returned. I did as I was told; then waited almost an hour before I was paged to the hotel information desk. There, I was told to use the courtesy phone again. I dialed the room number and was told to come up to a different floor and room number. Nearly drenched with sweat, I knocked on the door as I noticed that the room was next to a storage closet.

After a moment, a short elderly man with a ruddy face opened the door to welcome me. Wearing a black suit, white shirt, and a black bow tie, he looked like something out of a 1930's spy movie. Shaking my hand, he told me his name in a clipped British accent. Overly polite, he told me to sit in a chair facing a mirror on the wall adjoining the storage room. When I noticed a large black suitcase on the bed, I immediately felt ill at ease and sorry that I came.

Sitting opposite me, he spoke in a friendly yet forceful manner. With a half smile on his face, he remarked that his organization was greatly interested in me. At the conclusion of a flurry of personal questions about my life, relatives, and hobbies, I mentioned that there might be a problem with a background check due to the activities of my great-uncle in the Soviet Union. Smiling, he waved his hand and told me not to worry. As it turned out, the government was interested in me because I speak ten languages. They were looking for a linguist like myself who could travel the world posing as a businessman to gather information from specific people. Or, I might be used as an embassy employee posing as a state department agent to find out information from within an embassy. I would be given the best of everything. In other words, it would be a life that was the next best thing to being rich. Either I would receive two years of all expense paid training at their school and then be moved to Virginia, or I would be trained in a safe house in an undisclosed location so that no one would see me enter their school.

At the end of our meeting, he stood up to shake my hand and gave me a list of suggested reading material. Then, he told me to take an eight-hour written test the following weekend at the New York Institute of Technology. Stating that it was by invitation only, he handed me a numbered pass, looked me in the eye with an icy stare and said coldly, "Do be there!"

Leaving the city, I headed straight home. My head was pounding, my mouth bone dry, and I could not stop perspiring. For some reason, I had an urge to go to the beach. I packed up my family and headed for Smith Point Beach on the South Shore. While there, I remember looking east along the shore toward Montauk Point.

14

SECURITY RISK

The test was given in a building at the far end of the campus on the second floor. I was among the first to arrive, and only one door was open. As others arrived, I noticed that no one spoke to anyone else, as instructed. There were about twenty of us, all twenty-five to thirty-years old and all mostly white and male. Each segment of the test was timed and proctored by a different person. We were not allowed to ask any questions. Subjects included math, current events, science, and even music. There were multiple choice, essay, logic, and fill-in-the-blank questions as well as story problems. Grueling and torturous, the test started at 8:00 A.M. and did not end until 4:00 P.M. with only minor food and bathroom breaks.

When I left, I could barely drive. My entire face was sore and contorted. I had an amazing migraine headache, and my joints were in excruciating pain. Even my teeth and jaw hurt so much that I could not speak. I felt like I had been hit by a train. Almost forty-eight hours passed before I began to feel normal.

A few weeks later, I received another phone call telling me that I did so well that they wanted me in Washington immediately. Once there, I would stay in a safe house hotel. I would be given a polygraph test, go to

Langley for a mental evaluation, and given another physical examination. I made reservations to fly there the following week.

The TWA flight from LaGuardia to Washington's National Airport was uneventful but quite beautiful as we passed over an exceptionally clear Chesapeake Bay with its shimmering blue water and curvaceous shorelines. I took only carry-on luggage because I detest waiting at airport carousels. When the plane landed, I walked through the gate area, and directly into the lobby. From there, I was unceremoniously ushered to a waiting line of taxis and whisked into a cab. It started moving even before I told the driver where to take me.

The driver was a man of East Indian descent. Wearing a big smile, he was overly friendly as he asked about me. Excitedly, he told me that he also was from Long Island and still had family there. When I mentioned that I particularly enjoyed the parks and beaches, he replied that his favorite place was Montauk Point and that he found the Native Americans there to be very interesting. At this point, I realized that we were leaving the D.C. area and heading into Virginia. I had not even told the driver my destination! I asked him how he knew where I was going. Suddenly, he acted surprised and asked me which hotel he should take me to. Again, I never told him that I was headed for any hotel.

I remarked to the driver that I had reservations at the Holiday Inn in Tyson's Corners. Nodding, he said little the rest of the trip. Years later I read that this same hotel was a CIA safe house and had been used to entrap and capture a Soviet double agent.

As instructed, I checked into the hotel under my assumed name, Nathan Diton. The hotel was several stories high. My room was about halfway up. When I saw that my room was adjacent to a broom closet/supply room, I laughed to myself and realized that I was being observed at every moment. I became a bit annoyed when I saw that even the bathroom mirror was on the wall next to the supply room. Seconds after entering my hotel room, the phone rang. A male voice welcomed me to Virginia and told me not to leave the hotel premises for any reason. I would receive a call early the next morning regarding the polygraph exam.

Next, I went downstairs to use the exercise room and pool. Oddly enough, for a hotel of this size, I saw only five other people in the entire building. In the hotel restaurant, I was again astounded to see that I was the only dinner guest. Served by a beautiful Arab woman, she told me that she was from Jordan. We talked about the Middle East for awhile, and I told her about my trip to her country. Feeling exceptionally awkward and lonely, I ate quickly. As I prepared to leave, a group of three Japanese men sat down at the bar. They seemed to be in good spirits, laughing and joking in Japanese. Getting up, I paid my bill and returned to my room in anticipation of a long, lonely night.

After my shower, I turned on the television, checked to make sure the door was locked, and went to bed, tucking the covers under my chin. Then, I turned on a lamp by my bed. That was the last thing I remember until hearing the telephone ring. I was lying naked and face down on the bed. My rear end was raised higher than the rest of my body and all the bedding was on the floor. The television and lamp were still on and the clock on the nightstand read 8:00 A.M. I never woke up that late! I answered the phone in a daze. A different man's voice told me to have breakfast and be at another room by 10:00 A.M.

As I hung up the phone, dozens of questions raced through my head. How did I lose my clothing? How did I get from nine o'clock at night to eight o'clock the next morning in zero seconds? Why did my head hurt? Why were my testicles burning and my rectum sore? Frightened and jittery, I wanted to run — but where would I go? My eyes were sore and my chest pounded. Was something in last night's poached salmon?

After a light breakfast, I walked around the perimeter of the hotel to pass the time until my next meeting. As I walked, flashes of a beautiful, tall blond woman passed through my mind. I saw her strapped down on a gurney. I was strapped down next to her. Every time these pictures flashed in my head, I felt pains in my stomach as well as a feeling of helplessness and being surrounded by blackness. In addition, I smelled gasoline fumes that made me sick. Confused, my head was spinning. Was I just nervous? Again, I wished that I was home.

At 10:00 A.M., I went to the designated room where I was met by a pleasant dark-haired woman who was setting up equipment. In her late 20's, she was slightly plump but very friendly as she told me about the proceedings. She would go over all of the questions with me beforehand so that there would be no surprises. They wanted me to pass this test. She said that it would take about two hours. I sat on a chair while she sat on the bed and read the questions to me that I would be asked. Some were simple, such as questions about my background and likes and dislikes. Others were pointed and personal. They concerned my sexual appetites and the way I used the bathroom! I was perspiring profusely when she finally hooked me up to begin the polygraph test at 11:30 A.M. Around noon, I glanced at the clock again.

The next thing I remember was looking at the clock. It read 3:00 P.M. In shock, I realized that I recalled nothing of the past three hours! The woman was unhooking me as she remarked how much I would enjoy living in Virginia. She told me to wait for fifteen minutes after she left; then clean the room to look like no one had been there. Finally, I was instructed to drop the room key off at the front desk, return to my room for instructions, and talk to no one. I did as I was told.

At 4:00 P.M., a man dressed in a suit came to my room. He reimbursed me for my airline ticket and told me that I would receive instructions in the morning about going to Langley for the mental evaluation. Preferring at this point to watch television and read, I did not sleep that night. In the morning, I received a call instructing me to return to New York without explanation. I took the first flight back. A few weeks later, I received a phone call at work. A male voice told me that my application process had been stopped due to a security risk. When I pressed for details, they only told me to try again in a few years.

15

I MEET PRESTON

In retrospect, the next part of my life feels like it was only a dream, yet it really did happen. It is still difficult for me to discuss. Everything began when my employer moved, and I decided not to go with them. Looking for alternative employment, I saw an 800 telephone number on the back of a local food distributor truck that I followed home from work one day. The number stayed in my head for weeks until I finally called them.

Hired immediately, I started working there within two weeks. I was thrilled to be so close to home that I could even walk there if necessary. From the first few days that I began my new job, I realized that everything just was not right. The owners were four brothers, and they were mean and nasty. They had private meetings amongst themselves and gave out harsh orders to their employees. I soon found out that they were underhanded people with high connections to organized crime, banking, politicians, and big business. On different Sundays, when no one was around, they had meetings with the head of a teamsters union who was a known crime figure. Once in awhile, the chairman of a large local bank flew in by helicopter to talk to them after business hours. Large sums of money were deposited in their commercial accounts. They also had strange deals

MONTAUK: THE ALIEN CONNECTION

with other distributors and manufacturers that not even their big eight accounting firms could figure out.

Shortly after I was promoted to controller of the company, one of the brothers began asking me to impersonate him on the phone with various vendors and with his daughter's school. All of the brothers had spoiled children with psychological problems. I was also asked to write letters to other businesses under the guise of being one of the brothers. I did not like doing these things, but I also did not want to lose my job. The brothers were wealthy, powerful, and often made threats against their enemies as well as each other. One of the brothers purchased Ferdinand Marcos' home on the South Shore of Long Island. Another one of the brothers built a huge home on the North Shore. Unbeknownst to me at that time, Duncan Cameron, the lead psychic of the Montauk Project, was hired as one of the carpenters!

One day, when I had been employed there for about two years, my boss asked me to answer a phone call that he did not want to take. When I asked him what it was about, he replied that it had to do with stocks and the market. He further told me to do whatever the man wanted. He then left the building. Subsequently, the call was transferred to me. A strange voice told me a name and a company in Colorado that sold penny stocks. When I explained to the man that my company did not invest in them, he changed his tone. I felt my mind become foggy. All I can recall is that it involved a company in Austria that sold special storm and earthquake-proof building materials. They needed investors for their upcoming move to the United States.

What followed for the next eighteen months was disturbing, mind-boggling, and horrific for me and my family. Somehow, I managed to buy this stock with corporate funds by using a corporate seal that was kept in a safe to which I did not have the combination. During the ensuing year, I apparently embezzled over three-hundred-thousand dollars! I use the word "apparently" because I have no recollection of actually doing this. Even the F.B.I. determined that the handwriting on the checks was not mine. Additionally, no one could find evidence in the computer that I entered in the codes for the checks.

Now, I am convinced that I was physically manipulated in some way to commit this crime. I do remember going to the local banks to open checking accounts for fictitious corporations. I also used some of the funds for myself because someone told me that I could. Some of the checks were even stamped by the brothers themselves. Although they had full charge of the books, the auditor and the accounting firm said nothing for over a year. The fictitious accounts were opened in the same branch bank that my employer used. If these activities were against the wishes of my employer, how could I have gotten away with the "embezzlement" for so long?

Thinking back to that part of my life, I felt like an observer who watches someone from a distance rather than as an active participant. At the time, I remember thinking, "This has to stop, but I just cannot!" I felt as though I could not control my actions or my thoughts. Only thoughts of my children stopped me from running away. Some days, I even thought of killing myself.

Once, when I went to open some of the fictitious accounts at the Long Island Savings Bank, I remember a long line by the desk. A red-haired woman stood up from behind the desk and walked over to me. Speaking in a thick Russian accent, she instructed me to go in front of everyone and sit by her desk. She told me to come directly to her for all my banking needs. Even though I needed proper identification papers to open these bogus accounts, she waived them. She even deposited the checks for me while I waited. Looking at me strangely, she remarked that she was from Leningrad and proceeded to tell me about my great-uncle and his family in the Soviet Union. She said that my great-uncle made up the name Sverdlov and that it was not his birth name. He also ordered the deaths of the Czar and his family in Yekaterinburg. She explained that is why they renamed the city Sverdlovsk. Her husband was a coordinator for Radio Free Europe. She told me that he might be interested in interviewing me for a show scheduled to be broadcast to Russia. Oddly, I seemed to see this woman everywhere I went in the following months. Even her car, with the Russian flag on the bumper, often appeared just ahead or behind me in traffic. One day, after my legal problems began, I went to the bank to close out the accounts. Another woman banker angrily told me that my Russian friend was no longer working with the bank. She would not disclose any more information, and I never saw her again.

During this same time period, I became obsessed with UFO's and aliens. They were in my dreams almost every night. When I saw an ad in the local paper about forming a support group for abductees, I called immediately. The woman who called me back seemed friendly and outgoing. Because my home was centrally located on the island, we agreed to use it as the weekly meeting place. Although this greatly upset my wife, I persisted.

I became obstinate and aggressive, especially toward my family and friends. They all have since remarked that I seemed to simply change overnight into a very evil person. Strict with my children, I yelled and screamed at them constantly. I wanted their toys picked up and put away, even while they still played with them. Of course,

I now realize that set the future stage for years of therapy for them. Even my own mother started to call me Hitler. At the time, I kind of liked it.

When I realized that the support group was an avenue for borderline lunatics to parade through my house, I decided to end it for awhile. Our last meeting was a trip to see *Communion*, a movie I thought was a farce. Then, on the night of the Avianca crash on Long Island, the group leader called. She wanted to visit because she had "figured the whole thing out." In the living room, she leaned forward, grasped my hands, and started to speak. I was excited to learn the answers I had waited so long to hear.

She said, "It's all Satan. Satan runs through our minds and tells us false stories. He makes his demons look like aliens in order to fool us. I went to my church, they sat me in a chair, and started to pray. Strange voices came out of me and I spoke in tongues."

When the church members finally declared her cleared, they went to her home and destroyed all of her UFO tapes, books, and notes. Thanking her for coming, I quickly led her to the door. I thought that she was nuts; even nuttier than people thought I was. But at least, it was over for her. She would never have another question or doubt. She had found her answers.

During the time of my insanity, I received a phone call at work from yet another man at home on a Saturday. Speaking with a thick French accent, he said that he worked for yet another stock company, this time in New York. When he told me that he was from Madagascar, my brain fuzzed over again! I cannot remember the conversation, except I do recall that I agreed to meet his wealthy friend, a former NASA employee.

The following week, a tall, thin man from the "Real World One" company came to my office. John Giovanelli,

Jr. was peculiar in several ways: he always spoke in a soft monotone voice; his skin was extremely pale; and regardless of the outside temperature, he always wore long sleeves and a sweater. Over the next year, this man convinced me to go into business with him and build affordable housing on the east end of Long Island. After giving him several thousand dollars, he disappeared off the face of the Earth.

On one occasion, the man from Madagascar, accompanied by his Cuban wife, came to my house with plans to open a business in Madagascar. Later, when I met him in the city, he brought a girlfriend from Washington, D.C. She worked for the Organization of African States and would be a good contact with the African countries, he said. To make a long story short, this man was arrested for trying to buy green cards and then propositioning the female prosecutor. What a group of friends I had!

In the meantime, my problems continued to escalate. Helicopters were practically landing on my roof on a daily basis. My abductions and nightmares about being taken underground increased to the point where I was afraid to stay in my own home. On Valentine's Day of 1990, I called the Federal Aviation Authority to complain about the helicopters. The very next day, I received a call from the Federal Postal inspectors. They told me that I was the target of an investigation. My heart dropped as my life flashed before me. This was it. Everything was going to end now. I was relieved and depressed at the same time.

My sister's divorce attorney referred me to a criminal lawyer who promised to get me off easy. At the time, I had no conception of the legal system, and I trusted my lawyer. Even though I paid him a large sum of money, I soon realized that he was not on my side. In fact, he and the prosecutor were friends who had worked together in the

Drug Enforcement Agency. After taking two polygraph tests, I was told that I passed one and failed the other. The investigators told me that they thought I was guilty, but I knew that I was manipulated. Every time I tried to tell them my side, they literally told me to shut up.

During this awful time, I cloistered myself at home. I was even afraid to go near the windows because I knew the house was being watched. Sometimes, when the phone rang, I heard only breathing or the whirring of a computer. One day, when I reluctantly answered it, I heard the voice of a woman with a heavy Brooklyn accent. Telling me that she was a friend of a friend, she wanted me to write my story so that it might help others. She then invited me to her home in Brooklyn to meet a man named Preston Nichols. He was giving a speech about the Montauk Project. My blood ran cold at the mention of Montauk, but I agreed to come. Afterwards, she arranged for Preston to drive me home. Shortly after, this woman sent me a tape about UFO's and Montauk. She also included a box full of Majestic-12 papers. There were maps of underground tunnels, alien autopsy reports, and even a photo of a dead alien! Why was she sending all this to me?

The meeting took place on the night of my tenth wedding anniversary. My marriage was so bad that it really did not matter; it even seemed fitting that I not be home. I was absolutely shocked at the number of people who attended. I never realized how many others were interested in this subject, nor did I ever imagine that anyone was actually giving lectures on this topic. The hostess was amicable but money-oriented. Telling me that she was coauthoring a book, she also shared that she channelled information from an entity who had been with her since childhood and that a reptilian being had an amorous interest in her.

On the ride home, Preston told me more about the Montauk experience, adding that he believed I was one of the "Montauk boys." These were the children used in the heinous mind control and genetic experiments, as well as time-travel work. As he spoke of specific events at Montauk, goose bumps and chills ran up my spine. He seemed to be telling me about my own life. I wondered how he could possibly be aware of my experiences. Continuing, Preston told me that I was not alone. There were others like me. I wanted to meet some of the others as proof to myself that I was not insane. The following week, we arranged to meet at my house when my wife would be gone and the children asleep.

When Preston arrived, we went to a private room. Nervous, I did not know what to expect. As soon as Preston began his psychotronic/Wilhelm Reich proce-dures,* I immediately went into a trance. My body became rigid. I could not speak as I actually began reliving experiences. I heard Preston's voice as he asked questions, but I could not respond. At no time did he tell me what to see or experience.

Suddenly, I was a young teenager strapped down to a table in a brightly lit room. Men dressed as doctors worked on me, but I was awake and felt pain as I heard their words. They spoke of using me for genetic material before putting something into my groin area to make me extremely fertile. Next, I flashed to a scene where I was surrounded by little greys who asked me to perform some kind of function, but I do not know what that was. At times, I felt like I was floating through brightly colored energy

---

* These procedures involve increasing the orgone energy (life energy) in the body so that the mind can utilize it for psychic/hyperspace purposes. Some of this was detailed in the first two Montauk Project books. Psychotronics refers to the interface between the spirit, mind, and body with particular regard to the influence of technology.

fields; sometimes swirling around in a vortex, then lifting upwards at tremendous speeds. Finally, I felt myself come back to my body, but I could not move it as I slumped over in a standing position with my hands touching the floor.

I heard Preston trying to wake me up, but I still could not move. Ever so slowly, my body started to respond again, but it was extremely cold. I felt dizzy and disoriented. After I told Preston as much as I could, he informed me that during the session my body became as stiff as a board. He said that I had acted like someone who had been trained to do this for a very long time.

While I was looking forward to my next encounter with Preston, I was also anxious about opening my locked memories. As I opened the front door, Preston came in with Al Bielek (Duncan Cameron's brother from the Philadelphia Experiment) right behind him. Following behind Al, I saw a face that hurled me back to my childhood days when I saw that laughing face in my second-story bedroom window. How could this be? Who was this nightmare that had come to life? Staring in disbelief, Duncan Cameron smiled and walked into my hallway. MY GOD, this was the face of the man who had been in my window! It was real...not a dream! This was the same face that had terrorized my teenage years!

As I was introduced to Duncan, I felt an electric current shoot through my spine. This was a sensation that I would feel many more times as I relived my repressed memories. It was the feeling of an electric prod used at Montauk to bend the wills of the children into submission. Friendly and respectful, Duncan was not at all what I had expected. Rather than the evil mentalist that I had experienced in my teenage nightmares, he was soft-spoken and polite. I was thrilled to finally be able to speak without shame about my experiences to people who understood.

Plus, they could provide documentation that would either prove or disprove these experiences.

That night, the session was most interesting. After I was entranced, a small white being, who looked like a typical grey, entered my body. Speaking at first in a strange language that only Duncan understood, it then spoke in English as the tone became more ominous. This being said that it had every right to take possession of my body because I was one of them! Challenging this remark, Preston said that I was a human being with a soul from God, and no one was allowed to use the body except Stewart. The entity cursed Preston and called him "Pressed On." It said I worked for them and was carrying out a mission vital to the success of their program on Earth.

Both Preston and Duncan saw the physical shape of my body change as if it were a grey alien body. The outline of my face similarly changed. Then, the being started to move my body. Getting up, it walked around while making nasty comments about those present. Although my eyes were closed, my body walked around the room as if it were wide awake.

When Preston started to ask questions about their agenda, the being hesitated. Next, an extremely powerful entity literally pulled the grey from my body as it took over. Identifying itself as a Draco commander, it gave its name as "Gengeeko." Preston immediately understood the Draco to be powerful, reptilian warriors. The creature told Preston that an invasion force was on its way to Earth and that nothing could stop it. The moon orbiting the Earth was their first craft. It had arrived here aeons ago to control the planet. After creating the Lemurian civilization, they had been removed from the Earth by the Atlans and the descendents of the disbanded Lyraen Empire with the help of the Pleiadians. Now, the Draco were returning to reclaim the Earth and use it as a military base for entry into the rest of the galaxy. At this point, I realized that this was why so many races were interested in the Earth. If this planet falls, then the rest of the galaxy is in danger.

The Draconian then stood up and rasped a warning at Preston not to use his equipment or Pleiadian contacts to try to stop them. Next, he physically attacked Preston! Both Duncan and Preston had to restrain this being in my body until it finally sat down and resumed its speech. Claiming that humans were weak, it said that humans needed the order that an invasion would bring. This way, the invasion would benefit everyone. The Draco would receive the raw materials, workers, and food that they needed for their invasion into the rest of the galaxy. The Earth would be protected forever by the Draco Empire.

Our leaders were well aware of the impending invasion, gradually preparing the world population via television shows and movies. Even rulers in some countries were humans with Draco soul-personalities. The reptilian within my body expanded upon his ideas by saying that the United Nations would be the forum for a central planetary government. United States leaders were in league with Draco allies without realizing it. Some of the leaders of this planet had prepared escape plans to Mars where equipment was already being activated, as well as to other planets and moons in this solar system. Mars has a huge underground facility built by the Sirians over 500,000 years ago.

Gengeeko said that my body could be used since I was once an ambassador to their home world from the Ohalu Council, the ruler of the Sirian star system. I was neutral and not really concerned about who was in power. This is basically true for me; I am not a political person. My main interest lies in helping individuals to advance their souls and minds. Continuing, Gengeeko stated that I was created with alien genetics and that my soul-personality was not human nor from this star system. This explains why I have so many mental abilities that are considered unconventional on Earth.

When I came out of this trance several hours later, my body was dehydrated and extremely cold. Disoriented and confused, I did not return to normal for almost two days. In addition, I suffered rectal bleeding, shortness of breath, and severe shivering. Overall, it was not a pleasant experience.

16

IN THE CARIBBEAN

The night after the event with Gengeeko, I started remembering details about a cruise I had taken with my wife a couple of years earlier. On the second day, as we sailed along the coastline of Cuba, a strange feeling came over me as I viewed the tall mountains and small fishing villages. Nearing Havana, I took pictures which, when later developed, showed only fog and smoke. I felt as if I was there for a reason, and I knew that I was going to be a part of something that was going to happen in Cuba the very next day.

That night, it was rainy and the sea slightly rough. During my sleep, I was awakened by a voice calling out the name, "David." Opening my eyes, I asked my wife what she wanted. There was no reply, but hovering over my wife's bunk was a beautiful woman dressed in a flowing white robe that seemed to blow with an imaginary wind. Holding her hands out pleadingly to me, she again called out the name "David." Suddenly, she became smaller and quickly floated backwards out the closed window. I then realized that I was drenched in sweat and felt sick to my stomach. The cabin was pitch black. After falling backwards onto my bed, I seemed to go into some sort of trance.

The vision of an airliner taxiing down a runway appeared before me. I was standing beside the fence of the airport perimeter with several other people. My hands held a device that emitted a wave of energy. As the plane became airborne, I was told by a person standing next to me to shoot it down. Mentally, I turned on the device. Glowing red, a beam of light shot towards the plane which was now obscured by rain. Then I heard an explosion accompanied by a man's voice saying, "Good job!"

The next day, I awoke with a headache and stomach ache. My wife had no recollection of my trying to call to her the night before. In fact, she stated that she had slept rather soundly.

That day we arrived in the Yucatan in Mexico. We took a wonderful trip to the Mayan ruins. I was impressed by the stone carvings of flying serpents and beings who appeared to be at the controls of spaceships. Climbing the steps up the steep pyramids was exhilarating. Returning to the ship, I picked up a local newspaper in the main lounge. In astonishment, I saw a picture of a chartered airliner which had crashed at the Havana airport the night before in a rain storm. Everyone on board was killed. Most of the victims were Italian tourists returning to Rome! What had I done? How was this possible? Had I been at that airport in my vision...or was it more than a vision?

I could hardly speak the rest of the evening. The following day, I argued with my wife as we sailed through the Cayman Islands. That night, I was afraid to sleep; so on the night run to Jamaica, we went out for some night air. Walking on the top deck, the sky was clear and the stars magnificent. Starting to relax, I felt the tension leave my body. Suddenly, an arch of brilliant light flashed over the entire ship. Originating from the far south, it ended way to the north near Cuba. Everyone on deck stood mesmerized.

Then it happened again; this time in a bluish-green light. As most of the couples hurried inside, I remarked that maybe it was heat lightening. It really looked like a stream of energy. Peering over a railing in front of the ship, my wife and I saw that everything was completely black. Then, from our right, a fast-moving silver ball swooshed inches from our faces, crossed the ship, and continued over the sea. Looking at each other, I said, "Did you see that?" As my wife nodded in amazement, a second silver object swooshed in from the sea, hovered inches over our heads for a split second, and continued out over the sea. We both turned and ran inside!

Haiti was our next stop. While walking on the north coast, I was overcome with a flash of intense heat and light. I do not know where it came from or why, but after returning home, I came down with a severe case of radiation sickness. My skin turned red, I had high fever, and all my body's soft tissue was blistered. My throat closed up, and my lips were burned. I passed whitish paste from my penis. I could not walk, move, eat, or drink. Delirious and scared, I lost eight pounds each day. My doctor refused to touch me or even take samples of my body fluids. I was dying. He said that if I continued for three days like this without water, he would place me in a hospital in the center for exotic diseases.

Laying in bed that night, I prepared to die. I was so weak that I welcomed the relief. Closing my eyes, I waited for the worst. At this point, I knew that I would never make it to the hospital. When I finally opened my eyes, I was surrounded by greys. My blood flowed through tubes that had been placed in both arms. A silver sheet was draped over my body. Unable to move or talk, I simply did not care. At the same time, I flashed back to a memory of sitting on a table in a stark white room. Again, tubes were in my arms as I watched my blood flow through a machine operated by two small greys. Through a long narrow window in front of me, I saw white rocks and hills. Further beyond, I saw the Earth! I was in a room on the moon! As soon as I realized this, I woke up thinking how strange it was to have a flash of memory during a vision — or was it simply a vision?

Next, I noticed that my blisters and fever were gone! I was able to get out of bed! Looking in the mirror, I saw that my face had returned to normal. My throat was open and did not hurt as I gulped some much needed water. Even my urine was now clear.

Of course, no one believed me when I told them about my experience. I cannot explain what happened. All I know is that it is true. I have the medical records to prove it. Why I was exposed to radiation is beyond me. No one ever told me why. In any case, I do not ever want to repeat that suffering.

17

BREAKTHROUGH

The next time Preston used Wilhelm Reich procedures, he brought his tape recorder. An entity calling itself "Tubor" entered my body with such force that I shuddered hard and nearly fell to the floor. Claiming to be the Draco controller of a mission to prepare Earth for occupation, Tubor's main concern was other alien and human influences on the population that might thwart their plans. These reptilian beings were extremely nasty and hostile toward anyone who questioned them. Tubor commented that it was disgusted with my body and detested the way a human felt. Humans were considered to be weak, fragile, and too prone to emotional reactions.

Insisting that I had a contract with them which permitted them to use my body before their official arrival, Tubor said that I was also destined to be a liaison during the invasion. Using a human in this way would allow both sides to understand the mind-set of the other. I had supposedly agreed to this because I was once the Sirian ambassador to their home world as well as to Arcturus and a planet called Umo. As the Sirian ambassador, I had successfully negotiated a technology contract between the Draco and the Sirians. Sirius A agreed to provide the Draco with high technology in exchange for free trade and passage of their vessels anywhere within the Draco Empire. This contract upset the Orion Confederation because, being controlled by the Draco, they would never be free. The signing of this contract eventually provoked a war between the Orion Confederation and Sirius A which continues to this day.

Tubor also told us that the Montauk Project employed Sirian technology. The Draco observed all experiments but were especially interested in the ones that involved genetic manipulation. Because they are an androgynous race, the Draco are exceptionally interested in species that procreate sexually. Using sexuality as a means of programming people and gaining mind control over the masses was particularly fascinating to them.

Whenever Preston asked questions or stated an opinion, Tubor became angry. He called Preston "Pressed On" and referred to Duncan as "Dunk Can." At times, Tubor hissed and swung his arms toward them. Tubor even tried to hurt my body by hitting or twisting parts of it. About an hour later, another entity pushed into me and threw Tubor spinning away. After falling limp to the floor, my body then stood up again.

Claiming to be a Sirian, this being gave its name as "Mishka." He said that he forced his way into the body to show me how to deflect hostile use of my body. Since I had Sirian DNA, I could easily learn how to defend myself using my abilities. Mishka said that he lived on a large Sirian space station called Calumba which orbited between Earth and Mars. This station was designed to monitor interference on Earth and surrounding planets. The Sirians were independent and considered to be the merchants of the universe. With the highest technology available in their possession, many races came to them for help. Even all the weapons used by the Draco came from

Sirius. When Preston remarked that this made them guilty of hurting others, Mishka had an answer. He replied that without Sirian weapons, the Draco would use brutal force to overwhelm their targets. In this way, the Sirians considered themselves to be a mitigating force in the galaxy.

Over the next several months, Mishka, Mishka's assistant Marshak, Tubor, and Gengeeko used my body to deliver warnings and ultimatums. I was given information that the USSR was in league with the Draco and allowing them to use Soviet bases for advance operations. But, the USSR would eventually break up into smaller nations and disrupt the agreement. When this happened, I was told that this was a deception to lull the rest of the world into a false peace. The various Soviet governments were closely aligned with each other. When the opportunity was right, the Soviets would pounce on the unsuspecting countries. In this way, the Draco had a powerful ally on Earth to do their dirty work for them.

During one of the sessions, a deeply buried memory rose to the surface. I remembered lying asleep on my bed in that hotel room in Virginia when four men came through the door and injected me with something that completely paralyzed me. Wrapping my body in a canvas tarp, they put me on a cart and rolled me to the elevator. They put me in the trunk of a car and drove for at least two hours on winding roads that seem to go uphill. I remember exhaust fumes choking me, but I could not cry out.

When the car stopped abruptly, I was removed from the trunk. As I was taken into the vestibule of a large house with a stone front, I realized that I was nude. Next, I was strapped down on a gurney by uniformed military men who carried me down a long, curved staircase to a cold, stone basement. There I was transferred to a Y-shaped table where I was strapped down. Something was placed on both temples while something else that hurt was inserted into my rectum. A man in a medical coat then injected a long, painful needle under my penis just above the scrotum and said, "No one will find any marks here."

One of the military men called this man Dr. Hans. There were many other men in the room as well. I also heard the names Jim, Jesse, and Colonel. After putting electrodes on my nipples, penis, and scrotum, they injected something into my navel. I saw machines of all types, but I do not know their purpose. Then, I saw a door open in a stone wall and a little grey came through. As it touched me with a finger that felt slimy and dirty, I squirmed and tried to scream.

Someone said that I had to be returned to the hotel by 4:30 A.M. They agreed to take me back to my room via the kitchen. My next memory was waking up naked in the bed with my face down and my bottom elevated. Preston's opinion was that either they were trying to get information that was stored in my body cells, or they were storing information for future use. Either way, I did not care for the experience.

The sessions with Preston continued at my home once or twice a week. I needed time in between to relax and rest my body. In a way, immersing myself in the mundane experiences of my daily work was a welcome relief. My daily routine seemed to balance these bizarre contacts.

One night, I set my alarm for the usual time: 4:45 A.M. But, at 2:00 A.M., I awoke to the sound of the alarm ringing. Looking at my clock, I saw the alarm was still set. A voice in my head told me to quietly come into the living room. For some reason, I was not afraid nor did I feel that anything was unusual. Walking down the hallway, I saw that the living room was now bathed in a soft yellow light although no lamps were on.

Sitting in a corner chair, I waited. In the opposite corner, a swirl of dark blue light emanated from the ceiling until it reached the floor. Two tall, thin, powerfully built beings appeared wearing black capes that enveloped them from neck to floor. The capes had high, Dracula-style collars. Both had long bald heads with large blue almond-shaped eyes. Their noses and chins were pointed. As one being approached me, I noticed that his skin was extremely pale. About seven and one-half feet tall, he almost touched the ceiling. As he came closer, a swirl of letters and symbols flew around my head as the being said, "Now you will understand our language."

Identifying himself as "Mishka," he told me that he brought someone special who wanted to meet me. The other being then stepped forward. A little shorter, he was about six and one-half feet tall. His features seemed more human. Mishka said that he would leave us alone; then he disappeared with a blue flash. The other being came closer to me and held up his hand with five long fingers extended.

"Hello, Father," he said. Quite shocked, I asked him what he meant. Giving his name as Elsinob, he told me that his age was the equivalent of 400 Earth years. In the mid-1500's, he continued, my soul-personality was a professor at a university in central Germany. At that time, I was abducted by greys. They took a genetic sample from me and sold my sperm to the Sirians who used it in a hybridization experiment.

A product of that experimentation, Elsinob had always wanted to meet his biological father. He had monitored my soul-personality through its sojourn in time and space until I was able to accept and understand what had occurred. His DNA was practically the same as mine because DNA forms around the soul-personalty's mind-pattern; therefore, he calls me "Father." He also wanted me to know that he appreciated my contribution to his creation. Telling me that our minds were linked, he said that one day I would know my mission with him on this planet. Currently living on Calumba, the Sirian space platform between Earth and Mars, he travels to Sirius and other worlds when necessary. Our home world is called Khoom. Even though it is now covered in ice, it is still exceptionally beautiful.

Sirian women, he continued, were much smaller and thinner. With their own sub-society, they did not often travel through space. He told me that my testicles were implanted with a device to increase sperm production and make me extremely fertile. Many races were interested in me for my genetic material. Although he was proud of this, he said that I should no longer allow myself to be used indiscriminately.

The rest of the conversation involved information about the Sirian interest in Israel and the Jewish people. The Jews, he said, were created as a joint effort between the Sirians and the Draco. The genetic stock came from the Hebrews, a race of Sirian origin. The Ohalu Council, comprised of the leaders of the Sirian civilization, provided the Torah (the first five books of Moses, i.e., the Old Testament of the Bible) with its coded information that I would learn to decipher. In fact, the Ohaluans are non-physical beings who remain in hyperspace. The Sirians are their physical descendents. Ancient Hebrew is the language of this council. A holy language, it comes directly from the Mind of God. Each letter is a symbol, number, archetype, and geometric shape that is used to translate from the spiritual into the physical.

In fact, each chapter of the Old Testament can be decoded to letter patterns. When recurring patterns are matched against one another, geometric shapes are formed.

These include a doughnut shape, diamonds, three-dimensional triangles, etc. When all the patterns are enfolded on one another, a tetrahedron is formed in multidimensionality. That is to say, the shape can only be demonstrated on paper by drawing a three-dimensional tetrahedron. However, its actual shape goes far beyond anything that can be shown graphically with current technology. All letters of the Hebrew alphabet can be seen within the shape of the tetrahedron.

In the ancient Hebrew alphabet there are four letters that have a stylized "crown" on top of them. No one knew why. However, if all of the other letters were somehow forgotten, except for those four special ones, by using these four, the tetrahedron could be reconstructed and all the other letters again found within the shape.

Scientists in Jerusalem and New York are only now realizing the information encoded within the Old Testament as they review it by computer and research the various letter patterns. What type of mind could have created such a timeless document? Certainly not a human one.

At the conclusion of our conversation, Elsinob told me to return to bed. Walking back to my room, I noticed that the glow suddenly stopped. The moment my head touched my pillow, I went into a deep sleep. At 4:45 A.M., the alarm rang. When I awoke, I remembered everything. That is when I became afraid.

18

CHRIST

Because I was now receiving information and memories on my own, I began to dislike the sessions with Preston. The Wilhelm Reich procedures became invasions of my privacy that I no longer needed or wanted. In the meantime, one of Preston's co-investigators gave me the telephone number of a middle-aged woman in New England who he thought could help me unravel my story. Abducted as a child, she was left blind as a result of the experiments that had been performed on her. Despite this, she was able to see mentally and used her abilities to deprogram others who had been traumatized by unconventional events.

During the several months before my sentencing that I worked with her, I learned a lot about myself and my abilities. Even when I went away to prison, I was on the phone with this woman every day for several hours at a time. We worked together to heal people from severe illnesses and accidents. I learned about my past and my future. I introduced her to a well-known football coach and to Preston. At first, they all got along; but as time went on, she began to separate me from my friends. She warned me that Preston and Duncan had a bad reputation in their field and disavowed any knowledge of the Montauk

Project or the Philadelphia Experiment. Because she had become my mentor, I paid attention to her and slowly disassociated myself with these people at her request. She began to tell me what to say, who to talk with, what to study, and how to act. Her phone bill and my "education" were paid for by the chairman of a large international oil company. He became my friend as I tried to heal him of a very advanced cancer. When he died, the payments stopped. I did not realize it at the time, but this woman was turning me into her own personal robot. She made promises that she did not keep.

The best thing that this woman did for me was to reintroduce me to Mia and my daughter who I had not seen in years. Mia immediately became my balance in hyperspace. My abilities soared as I was able to transcend time and space at will. I learned how to do absentee healing and to read minds. I could communicate with extraterrestrials whenever the urge struck.

Starting to feel arrogant and confrontational as my sentencing date approached, I fought with my parents and sister. My marriage was just about at an end. My children were afraid of me. Even I was afraid of myself. Thoughts of running away or killing myself filled my head. Asking God what my life meant, I decided that I would rather die than go to prison. So one day, I tried to drive my jeep off the road and into a tree. Pressing down on the accelerator, I aimed for a tree, closed my eyes, and waited for impact. After a few moments passed, nothing happened. I opened my eyes and found myself driving slowly down another road! How did that happen?

My anxiety brought on chest pains, so I went to my physician who prescribed Prozac, an antidepressant. As a result, I became anorexic and developed severe insomnia. My physician then prescribed tranquilizers for the night.

It was uppers in the day and downers at night. When I complained about it, he doubled my dosage. Soon, I was passing out from lack of eating. I lost touch with reality to the point that one hot summer day, I decided to go outside without a coat in order to freeze myself to death! When my wife dragged me back into the house, I ran into the bathroom where I began slashing my wrists with a pair of scissors. Breaking down the door, my wife pointed to my youngest son and told me to think about his future without me. Sobbing, I felt the lowest that I had ever felt in my entire life.

Shortly after that last incident, I was determined to leave this world. I refused to put up with any more human laws and deceptions. I had found out that my wife was working with the prosecutor as well as my own lawyer. They all wanted me to confess to committing the crime of embezzlement all on my own. The prosecutor and my lawyer even threatened to send her to jail as an accomplice if I did not say what they wanted me to say. Without my knowledge, they called my wife, scheming with her to pressure me into writing letters of guilt. No one wanted to believe what I was saying. After my lawyer read a manu-script that I had written about my life, he told me that I would go to prison forever if I published it. He said that I would be labelled an insane man and put into a federal mental institution. Whenever I went to his office, black helicopters literally hovered outside of his window the entire time that I was there.

Out of desperation and depression, I called Duncan and left a good-bye message on his answering machine. That night, my wife was going to be out late with her friends. After the boys went to bed, I would take my life. I called Duncan because I believed that he was the only one in the world who could understand my pain and suffering; to know what it is like to feel that you do not belong on this world; to be used by everyone and appreciated by no one. Finally, my nightmare would be over.

So, after the boys went to sleep, I kissed them goodbye. I considered what I was about to do. I thought about the pain and sorrow my parents and children would feel. I realized that my wife would be relieved that I was gone. I had always been an annoyance to her. Besides, I thought that she was having an affair with her boss.

After all of these considerations, I decided to proceed. My parents and sister would grieve for awhile but then would go on with their lives. Plus, they would have my children to love. The boys were young enough to forget me after some time had passed. I cried for what I could have been, and I cried for what I was. I had no guarantee that it would be better on the other side, but I prayed to God and His angels to protect and guide me. I asked for forgiveness, but I could not forgive those who had forced me to make this decision.

Opening a bottle of Russian vodka, I took my Prozac. I drank and took pills until I could not remember what I was doing. As I slowly slipped into a stupor, I put my head on the kitchen table. It felt cold, but I did not care. I am not sure how much time had passed when I felt heavy hands shaking me and voices of concern around me. I just wanted to be left alone. With blurred vision, I looked up to see Preston, Duncan, and Al Bielek standing in my kitchen. They were asking me a zillion questions. The evidence was on the table. They knew what I had done. Duncan had gotten home that evening to find my message. He rallied the others to my rescue.

They called the local hospital and the poison control center in Atlanta for help. I was conscious enough to tell them that I was not going to the hospital. I wanted them to leave me alone to die. They brought me into the den and put me on the couch. Someone brought me coffee and cake. They stayed a long time and spoke to me constantly. Slowly, I became increasingly conscious. I felt embarrassed, but some part of me was glad that they came. I realize now that my message to Duncan that day was an attempt to be saved. I really did not want to die, I merely wanted to change my reality. I wanted to know that someone gave a damn about me. I am grateful to those three men for coming to save my life. It would have been wrong to commit suicide. I would have missed so much.

In light of my state of mind, and the fact that my sentencing was coming up soon, Preston started coming over several times each week to help me download what was inside of me. Duncan called almost every day to make sure that I was okay. I started having visions of being in Jerusalem while Christ was walking to the Temple Mount and felt surrounded by His presence.

During one intense session with Preston and Duncan, I went into a Wilhelm Reich induced trance. Suddenly, I was strapped down on a table at Montauk while a man behind a glass partition electrically shocked my body. A man named Jesse (the driver of the car in Virginia?) was at my side injecting me with a needle. Above me, a rectangular screen flashed into a scene from an old city with people dressed in robes. Instantly, I zoomed into the picture at a tremendous speed. As I swirled, spinning around, I felt nauseated and dizzy. Just as quickly, I stood at the steps of a large Roman/Middle Eastern building constructed of yellow stone. There were columns in front. From a doorway at the top of the steps, a robed figure emerged. Instantly, I knew that this man was Jesus. A voice in my head repeated over and over, "Shoot him! Shoot him!" Along the side of my left leg, I felt a gun. I had never used one before. Despite everything inside of myself denying the order to shoot, I pointed the gun at this elegant figure. Looking down at me from the top of the steps, his eyes were calm and intense. He looked at me with total peace. Dropping the gun, I ran around the corner. I could not do it! I ran as if I had committed a crime. I had not, and no one followed. Was I running away from the spiritual side of myself? I knew that He forgave me.

Next, I found myself standing at the foot of a giant wooden cross. Looking up, I saw that same face peering down at me. As blood dripped from his forehead, I saw a gash in his right side. Suddenly feeling something in my left hand, I glanced down to see an empty glass vial. Glancing at my right hand, I saw a needle. Where did they come from? Intuitively, I knew that I had to fill the vial with this man's blood. Because I could not reach his head or side, I jabbed the needle into his left foot, or more specifically, his big toe. He did not even flinch. He just kept staring at me with his head on his chest. Moving the vial up to his toe, I filled it. He was bleeding profusely from the small wound that I had made. Looking up at his face, I saw him smiling back me. Did He know that I could not help myself? Did He know that this was the way it had to be? Inside, I wished that it were me on the cross instead of Him.

As I covered the top of the vial with my thumb, I instantaneously found myself standing in a cold, sandy desert with a tannish-red cast. Complete silence surrounded me. The sky was pinkish-red, and it was difficult to breathe in the atmosphere. In that moment, I knew that I was on Mars. Holding the vial in my right hand, I walked slowly as my shoes sank into the soft sand. At the top of a nearby hill, I saw a tall figure wearing a hooded robe that was tied at the waist by rope. The figure appeared grey against the pinkish-red background. I knew I was supposed to give it the vial. As I handed it over, the figure reached for the vial with its left hand and simultaneously pulled back the hood with its right hand. There was Duncan smiling at me! He put his arm around me as we walked toward a cave-like opening in the side of a rock wall.

Abruptly coming out of the trance, I felt tears running down my face. My body felt like ice. Duncan was comforting me as he was upset, too. I remembered that the blood of Christ was to be used to clone a body with an android brain. A duplicate of Jesus, it would have a government mind! The second coming would be staged! If a blood sample was taken from the figure, it would match the blood on the Shroud of Turin; thus leaving no doubt that this was the real Christ. It was a perfect plan to control the masses. There was no better place to hide this than at the Mars underground. The government had used this abandoned alien facility since the 1950's. The secret ship, *Aurora*, which was built by the secret government using technology obtained from captured and crashed UFO's, flew here every week from its base at Area 51 in Nevada.

The government also hoped to activate the defense systems on Mars and the Moon before the Draco invasion force arrived. This was a race against time. The government needed to have the people of Earth trust them and believe everything they were told. Who more would they trust than Jesus Christ Himself?!

19

POLITICAL AGENDAS

After remembering the Jesus episode, I began feeling guilty about all of the work that I had done for the government. I realized that most of the children with whom I had worked were either dead or in bad mental states. I also knew that those who had survived the torture and mind submission were "sleepers." That is, they were programmed to perform a specific function at a specific time. Only a specific event, word, or sound could activate the programming. Most of them were unaware of what was inside of them.

Some of these "sleepers" were programmed to act as vigilante groups to eliminate government opposition in a time of chaos. Others were to form satanic enclaves and bring in new blood for the experiments on an ongoing basis. Still others were programmed to create acts of sabotage against invading forces and disrupt communication systems wherever possible. I now realize that some of these groups have been prematurely activated, or perhaps are being tested in light of current events. I am sure that the programmers want to ensure that everything and everyone functions "properly." They do this by selecting a test group and transmitting a signal that activates a software sequence. These programs are buried in the subconscious minds of the hosts of the sequences. A given signal starts the software rolling. This is as if a diskette is temporarily placed into the computer drive of the mind and runs a new program. The individuals then act out the sequence. When this program is over, the diskette is removed and the original software begins running again. In some cases, the new software is activated prematurely. In other cases, it simply does not stop running.

This instigates specific events such as the Oklahoma City bombing, the explosions on Paris subways, attacks against civilians in the Middle East, and even the 1996 bombing of the Olympic Games in Atlanta. Taken singularly, these incidents mean nothing to the unsuspecting public. But, when all the events are viewed as a whole, one begins to see a rather ugly picture.

During my training, I was taught how to blend into any scene in any country. I was shown how to act, told what to say to avoid suspicion, and how to solicit trust from others so they would confide in me. I was even taught how to make myself an integral part of any organization and then disappear without a trace. In fact, I could have become an academy award winning actor. Actually, I was sent to Hollywood for a few days to play the role of a tourist on a bus. You would never believe how many confidences I created in only a few days.

Much of what I learned was drilled into my head by trainers and teachers during long hours of field training. This occurred primarily in the Middle East and Hawaii. For example, a young Japanese woman in Honolulu was posing as a tour guide and brought me to field agents in an apartment on Kuhio Boulevard. These agents were rather large Eurasian-type men with definite Japanese connections. For several days, they indoctrinated me about the flow of power from that region. Most of the money in the tremendous Japanese banks was actually funneled there from the U.S. and Great Britain through third channels to avoid identifying its source. The Japanese government however is controlled by Beijing, a city which still fancies itself as a dynasty from thousands of years ago.

The Chinese have always had secret but enduring ties to Jerusalem. Stories have existed of Chinese Jews since the time of the Roman invasions of ancient Israel. These Israeli refugees reached western China where they converted thousands of people. Although the Jews as a people are not known for proselytizing and converting, please recall that Solomon indoctrinated the Queen of Sheba into Judaic beliefs, creating an entire culture of Black Ethiopian Jews. Also, Jews usually refuse intermarriage unless the spouse converts. This is why there are so many blond-haired, blue-eyed Jews from Northern and Eastern Europe. This type of slow but methodical conversion occurred in Western and Central China over 1000 years ago.

By the end of the Middle Ages, there were supposedly millions of Chinese Jews who controlled most of the trade and commerce. This has been kept secret for generations. Even today, the Israelis secretly supply the Chinese with technology and advice.

In exchange, the Chinese will help with a planned invasion of the Moslem fundamentalist countries in the near future. They will attack from the east while the Israelis attack from the west. Hundreds of millions of Chinese could literally simply walk over Iran and Iraq without encountering much resistance. The Israelis could easily annihilate Jordan, Syria, and the Gulf states with nuclear weapons. They could also use the laser/sonic weapons given to them by the Sirians. The Moslem fundamentalists are the only resistance force that would be detrimental to the Draco invaders upon their arrival. Accordingly, the Draco want them eliminated to ensure a smooth transition of power.

Additionally, it is in the best interests of the Chinese and Israelis to keep India and Pakistan sparring with each other so that they will not be strong enough to take sides. This also explains the Chechen uprising in the former Soviet Union. These are clever diversions to weaken the armies of those countries so that when the time is right, there will not be any aid available to the Moslems.

I was also given information about the future of black Africans and their descendents. The black race was created aeons ago by a group of aliens interested in slave labor to work in the mines of Africa and Asia. Consequently, they have been enslaved for generations because they were genetically programmed to maintain a lowly status. In addition, the genetic memories of the other races perceive them as slave labor. This must change as the black race continues to advance into a higher level of existence. In fact, there is an entire planet available to them which will avoid outside interference in their progress. Leaders such as Louis Farrakhan and Jesse Jackson are preparing the group mind-pattern by teaching them that they are different and to remain separate from mainstream society. Personally, I do not support ideas of separation though I do believe that gross mistreatment of the black race has occurred. However, they may welcome the opportunity to develop their own unique civilization: one of beauty, naturalism, and abundance.

I also learned that there were originally twelve root races on the Earth at the beginning of life on this planet. What this means is that there were twelve original alien races that agreed to genetically manipulate and seed life on this planet as part of a great experiment. The purpose was to determine if all of the main frequencies in the galaxy could live together harmoniously or if they would destroy one another.

These twelve alien races monitored their contributions to the experiment over the millennia. Some lost interest while some completely altered their original ideas. In any event, the twelve races are returning to remove or aid their part of the project before invasion forces arrive on Earth and usurp all of the resources and people. The outcome of this invasion is yet to be determined.

Many of the original races keep bases in this solar system to watch the Earth. A Sirian base on Mars has existed for many thousands of years. The Amphibians have bases on Neptune and on Titan, a moon of Saturn. The Draco, who are the invading reptilians, have bases on Venus as well as under the Earth. The Pleiadeans have a base on a moon of Jupiter. Many others maintain platforms or stations in orbit around the Earth and other planets in this solar system. Most of them do not want to be discovered...yet.

In the early 1990's, I was contacted by a man in Los Angeles on behalf of Marina Popovich, the Soviet cosmonaut who was on a lecture tour in this country. Secretly, she was investigating the disappearance of a Soviet space-craft that had been on a reconnaissance mission to Mars. While approaching Phobos, a Martian moon, a strange-looking craft emerged from behind that moon, fired something at the Russian probe, and the ship was never heard from again.

Ms. Popovich knew my family history in Russia (remember, my great-uncle was the first president of the Soviet Union), and she knew about my background and training. She was interested to hear what I had to say about the missing Russian craft.

157

After several attempts to converse via phone, Marina was suddenly sent back to Moscow. To my knowledge, she never returned. I never had the chance to tell her that a Sirian vessel destroyed the Soviet probe on behalf of the U.S. government and the Israelis! Apparently, there were those people who did not want the world to find out about the monuments on Mars. These same people did not want the public to know that Americans were already working in the underground vaults on the red planet trying to activate alien technology. The Russians were working with beings from Tau Ceti who were the progenitors of the Slavic races. Although the Sirians, Tau Cetians, Russians, Israelis, and Americans were theoretically all working together against the Orion Confederation and the Draco Empire, each had their own agenda and withheld information from each other. The Americans and the Israelis wanted primary control so they can eventually dominate the world. They reasoned that the government with the most exclusive information and technology would win.

While in the U.S., Marina Popovich appeared on many television shows to explain the Russian awareness of UFO's and aliens. Unfortunately, her agenda did not fit in with the American schedule of disseminating information and disinformation. So, she was manipulated into the background and forced to return home. Only those people authorized by the U.S. government or those who control the government are allowed to speak about sensitive alien issues. These people can only repeat what they are told to say. Carl Sagan was such a man. So are some famous Hollywood producers who write science-fiction and political screenplays.

20

ABILITIES GAINED

My personal training, which increased my abilities to see auric fields and read mind-patterns, began when I was a little boy. After my first encounter with an alien being, I came away with a "knowing." I literally read the minds of other people who were near to me simply by looking at them. At the time, I did not realize that this was odd; I assumed that everyone did it. When I mentioned this to my mother and grandmother, they thought that I was making up stories. After that, I immediately dropped the subject and discontinued the ability.

My abilities seemed to increase with every alien encounter. By the time I was ten-years old, I could look into a person's body and see what was wrong with it. I was even able to look inside my own body and correct or heal any illness or pain. The knowledge seemed to come naturally, as if pre-programmed. This particular ability in healing and reading minds developed as a result of DNA sequences opening up in my body. This is a form of Kundalini activation which everyone goes through to some degree. To further explain, DNA codes are the instructions that tell your body what to do and be. Some instructions are running at birth. These dictate that you will have blue eyes, two legs, two arms, etc. Others activate later in life, such as health conditions, abilities to play music, sing, etc. Along the human spinal column there are seven main nerve bundles, called ganglions, which are esoterically called *chakras*, a word which means "wheels" in Sanskrit. They form along the "S" curve of the spine which looks like a snake. In Sanskrit, *Kundalini* means snake. Kundalini activation refers to the opening up of all the chakra centers along the spine. This results in activation of all DNA codes and sequences in the body. When activated prematurely, this can result in insanity, illness, and/or death.

During some of my alien abductions, I remember being indoctrinated in a variety of subjects, including the future of mankind. The rest was personal information involving mind control techniques and healing. These indoctrinations were not verbal. Usually, I was with a group of people sitting on curved benches in an alien craft. With our backs toward some type of large device and screen, we felt information flow into our minds. I did not consciously remember the exact details until I needed it. Then, the information flowed to the front of my mind. Certain triggers activated the information, such as a word, smell, color, picture, or an event. After the trigger, the sequence implanted in the brain activated, allowing me to access this knowledge at will. This experience is similar to finding a secret bank account that you never knew you had. Once you get the account number, you can make withdrawals at any time.

As I moved into my teenage years, the learning took on a different twist. Besides the alien indoctrination, I sometimes "dreamed" that I was in school but not the Earthly kind. While in the sleep state, I went to a large "hyperspace academy." Again, I was with a group of people being instructed on many topics ranging from healing, to world changes, to ancient history on Earth and elsewhere. Teachers tested us by scanning our minds to see if the information was assimilated. Usually, they were kind and caring, but sometimes they were firm and scary. For the most part, they were angelic beings; some appeared only as balls of light. Still others appeared extremely alien. A few looked human. These were departed people working their way up the ladder to a higher state of existence. These human teachers were usually watched by angelic beings who observed and graded them much like they did their students. This learning occurred for a period of about twenty years in my life.

In contrast, the government work was not pleasant at all. It even caused physical damage. At the Montauk installation, much of my training involved adverse conditioning. Using this method, the student is punished mentally and/or physically for a negative response or incorrect answer. My experience was that we (the Montauk boys), were all together in a cold, damp room. Stripped naked, we were literally hit and slapped by our commanders. If anyone was difficult during a training session, the teachers sometimes grabbed and squeezed our genitals very hard. They stuck us with sharp instruments and electric shock devices. This was supposed to teach us how to respond to interrogations and hide during a mission. At times, we were told about who we were as experiments and how we were carefully placed with our families. We were told that the U.S. was only a facade of the real power that existed and that we were expected to profess unconditional loyalty to this power behind the government. There were days when the entire lecture was given in another language like German, Russian, or Hebrew. I understood those languages, but I wondered if the others did. These were the easy days.

The really brutal lessons occurred when we were tied down to tables and given injections that altered our consciousness. While in an altered state, a device was put on my temples and genitals. I heard a whirring noise accompanied by a vibration that I felt all over my body. Usually this was painful and made me nauseous and afraid. I could not wait for these sessions to end. I now believe that information was encoded into my body cells for storage much in the same way that the aliens stored information in my mind. Through the use of Wilhelm Reich procedures, information was retrieved or added. In this way, the subject of an interrogation could not reveal any information unless the interrogator knew how to alter the subject's mind and activate the proper body cell sequences. Loading the information or retrieving it in this way was an extremely delicate maneuver because the wrong sequences could kill a person or drive them permanently insane.

At Montauk, I was also trained to feed energy and information to the psychic in the chair who was hooked up to mind control computers. While strapped into a chair, I actually listened to instructions via headphones. After I was linked telepathically and energetically with the psychic, communication then switched to purely mental instructions. I gave him energy directly from my mind and body in order to boost his power during an experiment. In turn, the computers boosted my own abilities, enabling me to travel astrally or into hyperspace. Over time, I learned how to do this at will and without the machinery or anyone else influencing my direction. Once my controllers found out about this, they kept me under close supervision. I was known to have a temper, and I used it to ruin their experiments through mental interference.

To prevent this, they assigned me to prepare the novice children. Their reasoning was to focus my abilities on people of their choice, rather than on them. I enjoyed this hideous job, I suppose, because I had that Nazi Johannes von Gruber inside of myself. I was very compulsive with the groups I was given to train. Starting out with young boys from four to ten years old, I quickly graduated to teenagers and young adults up to about twenty-five years old. Rarely did I see anyone over the age of twenty-five. Beyond that age, I was told that their mind-patterns were too fixed and that breaking them could quickly kill them. In fact, most of those boys died or went berserk. The stronger ones were sent to work as physical laborers for the greys on other worlds. Sometimes, their bodies were used in time travel experiments in order to align calibrations in the time fields. Losing a body was not considered a matter of any significance.

I was also given books and pamphlets to read about healing techniques and mind control. Then, I was given exercises to perform to test my abilities. I always passed with flying colors. In fact, it was through the manipulation of colors in the auric field that I did my best work. As a result of this experimentation and abuse, my eyesight and hearing diminished substantially. Instead of seeing and hearing like other people, my brain mainly picks up energy fields and colors. Rather than seeing the physical body of a person, I primarily perceive their mind-patterns and DNA sequences. Electromagnetic devices such as telephones, computers, and televisions amplify these energy fields and mind-patterns, allowing me to easily use them to do "readings" for other people.

The high rates of energy that flowed through my body damaged my nervous system, making me irritable and moody. My digestive system was severely damaged. I have ulcerations throughout my intestinal lining which causes internal bleeding and weakness at times. I also experience severe abdominal pain and massive head-aches. Not a pretty picture, but I can diagnose a patient from across the globe and feel an earthquake thousands of miles away. I can also communicate at will with beings in other dimensions or galaxies. Every ability has a price.

I must also add that the woman in New England (who spent several years deprogramming me) activated my entrained ability to read and understand mind-pattern archetypes. For this, I am grateful. I am also appreciative of Preston's procedures of retrieving my suppressed memories that also activated buried abilities. I do wish that there was an easier way for me to learn all of this, but it appears that my soul-personality chose this difficult path. I guess it was do or die. Therefore, I am happy that I survived to tell my story and use my knowledge to help others.

21

SENTENCED

Through all of this, my legal case was reaching a conclusion. After a two-year delay, my sentencing was set for February 27, 1992. My lawyer promised that in exchange for my coerced confession, I would receive a four-month sentence at a nearby country club prison camp and perhaps even half of that would be in a halfway house in New York City.

Two weeks before a sentencing date was set, I received information that a major power was planning to send a nuclear missile into a small Middle Eastern country. Through certain channels that I had in that country, I warned its government of the impending attack. I would like to think that I had some small role in saving the citizens of that land. But, it brought an unexpected tragedy to my personal freedom.

One week after I sent the warning, my lawyer told me that the sentencing had been moved up and to prepare a remorseful letter to read to the judge. I was in a state of shock because I had not expected the sentencing to come up so fast. Even though I had given him my last dime, this lawyer constantly hounded me for money. Repeatedly, he told me that he would continue to represent me even if I admitted to committing the most heinous of crimes. I just could not understand him. It seemed that the prosecutor, who was his friend, and the government had all teamed up with my wife to drain every last asset from me for as long as possible; then discard me when there was nothing left. I suppose that this is typical of the legal profession.

My lawyer also made me use an accountant who was a friend of his. He refiled previous years' income tax returns so that I could not be accused of income tax evasion. I claimed all of the money that was taken from the company for which I worked; even the amount returned to them. For this, I am forever under the harassment of the federal and state tax collectors. The picture emerges that I was supposed to be perpetually financially strapped and needy. Such a person would always be under the scrutiny of credit companies and collection agencies. Under these circumstances, a person could not afford to cause trouble for the government.

On the day of my sentencing, my parents, sister, wife, Preston, and Duncan all showed up at the court. The football coach who I had helped was also there. Because the docket was busy that day, it took a couple of hours to reach my case. The prosecuting attorney had previously agreed to ask the judge for leniency, but instead, he sent a proxy who refused to say anything on my behalf.

Finally, I was sentenced to thirty-three months in a federal prison camp and was asked to self-surrender in thirty days. The judge said that he did not believe in the sentencing guidelines and gave me the lowest end of the scale allowed. He said that his hands were tied and that I should appeal. Thank God there were witnesses to what the judge said because his words mysteriously disappeared from the court transcript!

I truly did not believe that I could survive that long in prison. My lawyer had obviously lied to me. In addition,

I later found out that he had withheld important information. For example, I was convicted under a new law that was in effect since 1987. It said that such sentences must be served for at least 85% of the imprisonment. Prior to 1987, one only had to serve 33.3% of the sentence. My lawyer falsely told me that I would be free in eleven months. In fact, I had to serve almost twenty-three months plus six months in a halfway house.

One week before surrendering, I called the federal marshals to find out where I was going. I was shocked when they told me Ashland, Kentucky! I had never heard of such a place. Besides, it was out of my federal region, and it is illegal to send a prisoner more than 500 miles from their home, unless it is for their protection or if they are a local threat. Obviously, I was being emotionally punished by being sent from the reach of my family. I realized that I would hardly see my children during this time. At that moment, I would rather have been executed. I hated the government and my lawyer with a passion. As difficult as it has been, I have since forgiven them as I know that, by their own actions, they have chosen a difficult path.

I booked my one-way flights for a Friday morning. I had to report to the prison camp by 2:00 P.M. or be considered an escapee. I was scheduled to leave Islip, New York on a flight to Pittsburgh, Pennsylvania; then transfer to a flight to Huntington, West Virginia. From there I would take a taxi across the river to Kentucky. Keep in mind that I had self-surrendered. At no time was I ever accompanied by law enforcement personnel of any kind; not even when I transferred to another camp or went to a halfway house.

My last thirty days of freedom I spent cloistered in my house. I stayed close to my children, ate my favorite foods, and drank a lot of vodka. On exceptionally depressing days, my mother and/or Duncan came over to comfort me. Most days, I just wanted to be left alone in a drunken stupor. I had been seeing a therapist for about a year, but he was more fascinated by my abduction stories while under hypnosis than he was in my mental status.

Much of the time, after the boys went to school and my wife went to work, I sat alone in the den and cried my eyes out until I did not think that I could produce any more tears. I worked almost daily on the phone with my female deprogrammer in New England. She was a tremendous comfort but also a tremendous controller. I now know she had ulterior motives. All the phone calls were paid for by a former chairman of Sunoco Oil who lived in Toronto. As was said earlier, this man was dying of cancer. As part of my deprogramming deal, I worked with him on his healing. A kind and generous man, I will always remember him fondly.

On the morning that I was scheduled to leave for prison, I had a nervous breakdown. I simply could not get out of bed! I refused to get up because I knew that I would never return to that bed again. I was certain that I would either die in prison or on the plane going there. My wife immediately called my deprogrammer and put me on the phone. She told me that I was to do great work in prison with men who desperately needed my help. She told me that prison was my assignment by the extraterrestrial with whom she worked.

There is a difference between aliens and extraterrestrials (ET's). An alien is a physical being who lives on another physical world. An ET is a being who lives in a higher state of existence, somewhere between physical and angelic levels. They are extremely advanced beings who can become physical when necessary. My Ohalu Council is comprised of ET's. My deprogrammer's group was called the EI's because they did not name themselves. Beyond the confinement of names, EI stood for "Extraterrestrial Intelligences."

She told me that when I looked out the plane window during my trip the EI's would give me a sign. Reassuring me that all would be well, she said that the plane would not crash since it would not be fair to the other people on board. She then instructed me to visualize violet hands holding the plane in the sky.

At the airport, I experienced the most traumatic moments of my life. I could not leave my children. I hugged them so tight that none of us could breathe. Staring at their innocent little faces, tears rolled down my cheeks uncontrollably. My heart felt like a lead weight. The deep sorrow was indescribably painful. I simply could not step foot onto the jetway to the plane. I must have caused quite a scene because my wife sharply yelled at me to go. I turned one last time to look at their sweet faces. I did not want to live anymore.

As the plane taxied down the runway, part of my soul took off from my body, never to return. At that moment, I imagined the pathos of the concentration camp victims as they said goodbye to their loved ones forever. Quickly, we were above the cold, snowy clouds and the brilliant sunshine jolted me back to my painful reality. I could not believe that I was voluntarily turning myself over to a jailer for something I was told to do for my government.

Trying to bury my thoughts in a book, I found that I could not concentrate. As I stared out of the window, I wondered when I would ever see my children again. I would miss so much of their young lives. How unfair. I had not taken anyone away from their families! Why was I punished this way? Then, I remembered the little Montauk boys. Some of those parents would never see their children again. Perhaps justice was done here, but I was not in control of that experiment. I, too, was a victim. Looking at the tops of the clouds, I saw how the sunlight shimmered on them. Then I saw the message. In tremendous block letters made out of the clouds themselves, I saw the initials "EI"!

As we landed in Pittsburgh, I seriously considered taking a plane out of the country. It was all that I could do to get on the flight to Huntington. After seeing the initials in the sky, I was more at peace but still emotionally overwhelmed by the situation. The short flight was bumpy, landing in West Virginia in the midst of a snow squall. It was like traveling backwards in time. I thought that I was in a movie about the Beverly Hillbillies. I simply could not believe that people like this existed except as cartoon characters. The culture shock was incredible.

The cab driver took me to Kentucky but first brought me to a state penitentiary on the other side of the road. I nearly had a heart attack thinking that this was the federal camp. He laughed when he realized his mistake. As we pulled up to the front entrance to the camp, I thought it looked like a high school campus. Then I rang the bell.

22

PRISON

A lumpy, middle-aged guard let me in and patted me down. He was friendly as he led me to a room where a female guard took inventory of my belongings. Again, I thought of the Holocaust victims. This time, I pictured the arriving inmates at Dachau or Auschwitz as their possessions were taken away from them and they were told to disrobe. Although it was not quite the same scenario, the premise was similar.

A male guard took me into a back room, stripped me, examined my body orifices, and issued me a green army-type uniform. I was then taken to another room for psychological evaluation. Apparently, someone in the New York prosecutor's office wrote on my paperwork that I was a suicide candidate. When the head psychologist came in to talk to me, I broke down uncontrollably. I could not speak or answer any questions. I could only think of the way my children looked when I left them in the airport. I did not think that I would ever see them again. Remembering my wife's promise to bring the children to visit me during their Easter vacation was my only comfort. This was only three weeks away.

After several hours of sobbing until exhaustion, I was taken into the camp population and introduced to another inmate who showed me around. Kind and understanding, he had a wife and daughter who he missed terribly. I went to my dorm and met the rest of my fellow inmates. They gathered around me like flies to honey. I could hardly understand their deep southern accents. They explained to me about the old law versus the new law. This was the first time that I had heard about it. Realizing that I would serve 85% of my sentence, not 33% like my bastard lawyer had told me, I was devastated even more, if that was possible.

These country boys had never seen a New Yorker before. As I was not supposed to be this far from home, they were sure that I was Mafia. Most of them were drug dealers or pot farmers with long sentences. To be in a federal prison camp, you have to have less than ten years left on your sentence. One prisoner was an old coal miner with black lung. He was given six years because he was visiting his son's property when the Drug Enforcement Agency raided it. There were also old men serving time for tax evasion. These were not violent people. Not one of them should have been away from their families. All should have been home with their loved ones, doing community service, and paying off their debts. Most of their marriages would dissolve. Most would never have a decent job again. I just could not believe how nice and good-hearted these men were. Why would our government spend so much taxpayer money to put them away?

I do not want this chapter to be a blow by blow description of my life in the prison camps. Suffice it to say that I learned a lot about the tactics of our so-called legal system. I saw men die for lack of medical care or from poor medical treatment. I saw the waste in spending for the fancy offices and resort-like recreation halls built for the administrators and the prison guards. I saw and ate from boxes of food stamped "Unfit for Human Consumption."

What I saw was a travesty of justice. True, most were guilty of white collar crimes, but most should not have been in prison! Their prosecutors were guilty of more heinous crimes than any of these men.

Because I was one of the few people with a full mouth of teeth, the camp dentist and his assistant posted my name for frequent appointments. They had never seen so many good teeth in one mouth. The dental assistant was a former neighbor of Billy Ray Cyrus, the famous country music star, so I spent hours with my mouth stuffed with cotton as I listened to her stories about him in her thick drawl.

Because of my education, I was quickly promoted to head teacher in the GED (General Equivalency Degree) program and even wrote my supervisor's weekly reports. I became the liaison between the camp and correspondence courses provided by local colleges. The head psychologist often asked me to counsel new inmates who were despondent. He thought that if I could make a life there, anyone could. I also joined a spiritual group headed by a Gideon chaplain who was a former helicopter pilot for John F. Kennedy. He visited the camp once or twice each week to help the inmates. I wrote an article for him that was published in the Gideon's magazine. I owe him a lot for his support and inspiration.

My proudest accomplishment was a course proposal I made to the camp education director. I developed a course to teach stress reduction and color therapy. It was approved, provided that I give a copy of each lesson to my supervisor, who I had befriended. My course was a huge success. I had the entire camp learning about the language of colors, archetypes, and mind-patterns. I did extensive dream analysis as well. Soon, inmates lined up outside of my cubicle at all hours in order to get private sessions with me. My bunkmate had to start making appointments for me and turning people away just so I could get some sleep. In my class, I helped fellow inmates cure themselves of all types of ailments including high blood pressure, obesity, diabetes, arthritis, and even the common cold.

At the same time, I spent hours on the phone every day with my deprogrammer. She was a big help to me when my stress was especially high. She asked me to use my mental abilities to heal patients of cancer, AIDS, and other severe illnesses. I was even doing work for Uri Geller, the famous Israeli psychic, at his request. I kept copious notes on all my patients so that I would know which mental work was most beneficial. Most of my research was done in the prison camps.

At night, and even in the day, I received messages from a council called "The Nine." Unemotional and matter-of-fact, they are nine aspects of the Mind of God projected into physical reality to help mankind. During my time in the camps, I heard from them almost daily; today, for some reason, I hardly ever hear from them.

I also received messages in the clouds. Whenever I looked up, I saw strings of hyperspace symbols or archetypes as clear as day. As soon as I read them, they vanished! To prove to myself that I was not crazy, I asked others to tell me what they saw. They were all dumbfounded as they saw the same cloud formations. People were even more amazed when I erased the clouds simply by looking at them!

Preston tried to send me messages by mail, but all I ever got were empty envelopes. All of the prison mail was read, and all of the phone calls were taped and monitored. Sometimes, I threatened the government on the phone, but no one took me away. Once, I even caused a small earthquake in Kentucky because I could not contain my anger.

What made me the angriest was the way the administration played with the inmates' minds. They promised things without ever doing them, put people in solitary confinement for stupid reasons, and raided cubicles to find contraband and lock a man up. It was bad enough that we were all there. Why make it worse with psychological warfare?

Another thing that made me angry was my realization that my wife and her boss were involved in some way. As soon as I left, she began inviting him to her home for dinners and going out on his boat. Next, she told me that he was going to buy our home. She started going out with her friends to nightclubs and bars and made it clear that I was no longer welcome. No wonder she worked with the prosecutor to put me away. The worst thing of all was when she reneged on her promise to visit me during the children's Easter vacation. I was devastated. Eventually, she did bring the children three times to Kentucky to visit me, and she also sent me money for phone calls and commissary purchases. However, like my dear grandmother used to say, "What good is the cow that gives a full bucket of milk and then kicks it over?"

To be fair, I do not blame her for not wanting to spend her life with me. We simply did not get along, and my abilities and beliefs got me into a lot of trouble. Although I wanted to keep trying for the children's sake, the relationship just did not work. She was helpful to me at times. For instance, she was instrumental in getting me a furlough transfer to another camp on top of a mountain in central Pennsylvania. The government wanted to send me to the Great Lakes area because at this point I was becoming too knowledgeable about the truth.

In the camps, we learned many things about the New World Order. For example, we learned that the prison camps were a model for what the world of the future would be like: forced labor for food and shelter. We learned that the large Japanese banks were a front for U.S. and German monies. We even learned that humans were already cloned and that some had been released into society for testing.

A friend of mine proved that the U.S. Postal Service was a front for a British bank and that it only costs two cents to mail a letter when the true legal code is imprinted on the face of a letter. We learned that foreign troops were secretly being trained in the U.S. for a time when all governments would defer to the United Nations as the sole government of the Earth. I even learned that AIDS was created in an American laboratory and tested in 1967 on an unsuspecting patient in a hospital in St. Louis, Missouri.

I learned so much that, before my transfer to Pennsylvania, I was locked in my supervisor's office for two nights and interrogated. I was asked many questions. Where do my loyalties lay? If the U.S. were invaded, who would I support? Would I use my abilities against the U.S.? Would I speak about what I had learned in public? Do I support an alien invasion of this planet?

I was threatened that if I spoke about my interrogation or my beliefs, the government would declare me insane and lock me up forever. I assure you that I answered all questions in a way that was beneficial to me! All of this confirmed my beliefs about our government. I also learned from the country folk in the camp that there were rebels in the mountains with vast arsenals. They are waiting for the day to revolt. That day is already upon us.

23

RELEASE

My trip to Pennsylvania was a brief taste of freedom. I took several buses through Kentucky, Ohio, West Virginia, and Pennsylvania. Remember, I was unaccompanied and could have escaped at any time. If I had done so, I would have been a hunted man and never able to return to my family again. During my overnight bus ride, I sat next to a number of upstanding American citizens. Smiling ironically to myself, I thought about their reactions if they knew that I was going from one prison to another. I looked as free as they did, yet I was still a prisoner of the U.S. government.

When I finally arrived in Minersville, I looked for a phone to call a cab. There were no public booths on the one street in town, so I asked at the local bank if they had a phone booth. The nice, middle-aged ladies behind the counter were overly hospitable and let me use their private phone behind the teller's counter. Asking if I was new in town, I replied, "Yes." They asked if I had a job, and I again replied, "Yes." When they asked where I was going, I told them, "To the federal prison camp up in the local mountains." The blood drained away from their faces. After all, they were alone with me in a bank, waiting for me to return to prison. I saw their visions of robbery and rape as they nervously and politely stepped farther away from me. Quickly, I added that I was a teacher for the prisoners, but by this point, they were wary of me. I took my luggage outside and waited for three hours for the only taxi in town.

This camp was very different from the one in Kentucky. It was more like a secret government installation. The Kentucky camp was old and in the middle of town. Children played across the street in the school yard. Here, there were only cold mountains and stark buildings. During my processing, I could tell that these guards were more apathetic than their southern counterparts and maybe even dumber, if that was possible. Perhaps it was all that coal in the ground that had dulled their senses.

Resembling an apartment building, the dorms here were more compact. These prisoners, mostly from the northeast, were unfriendly, arrogant, and wealthy. Many were lawyers and this actually pleased me. I felt that they were finally where they all belonged except that they were still breathing!

Because it was only a five hour drive from where she lived, my wife visited me more often. As the visits became more tense and argumentative, I realized that this marriage was not going to work out. When I thought of the children, it broke my heart, so I continued to persevere.

Once again, I quickly worked my way up to the position of head of the education department. I taught GED and ESL (English as a Second Language) classes. Most of my students were illegal aliens from Latin American countries. There were a few Arabs, Chinese, and Europeans. My lessons sometimes swerved from English to the truth behind the American government. Some of my students were former terrorists, so they were enthralled by what I told them.

When guards passed by, I quickly switched back to the lesson of the day. I was not supposed to teach classes without a guard or supervisor monitoring me. But, I became so trusted that I was left to devise my own lessons and agenda without prior approval. In fact, the main supervisor of the prison's entire educational department often asked me to review my own supervisors! Of course, some inmates interpreted this as a sign that I was really a spy for the administration. No matter. I had a good position and even wrote a book on how to teach GED and ESL which was quickly usurped by the government as their own. My coworkers were presidents and vice-presidents of major corporations. They were great advisors to me and I shall always remember them.

In Pennsylvania, I met my best friend, Peter Filatov. At first, I did not like him. I thought that he was aloof and arrogant, but he persisted. One day, I returned to the dorm to find my bed and belongings moved into Peter's cubicle. I was dismayed, but we stayed up all night talking and discovered that we had similar backgrounds. He was Ukrainian, and I was Russian. We both enjoyed exercise. We both felt betrayed by people we had trusted. I told him my story, thinking that he would be scared of my insanity, but he understood and wanted to learn more. So, I taught him about mind-patterns, color therapies, and dream analysis. Over time, he learned about my mental abilities and decided that I should write some of my information to share with others. At first I refused, but Peter was persistent.

The result of our collaboration is a book titled, *As Ye Sow, So Shall Ye Reap*, and its companion workbook, *The Healing of the Mind*. Peter and I have been best friends ever since. He was the first to suspect the motives of the woman who was deprogramming me. I refused to believe that she was anything but good, but Peter saw how she controlled and decided my every move.

One day, I received a letter from Peter Moon asking my permission to tell my story in the Montauk books. When I spoke to my deprogrammer about it, she exploded in anger and promptly dictated a letter for me to send to Mr. Moon telling him where to go. So, imagine my surprise when Craig, a fellow inmate, came down to my cubicle to get my autograph. In his hands was a book that his mother had sent him from Florida. It was the first Montauk book — with my name in the acknowledgments! Soon, I was a celebrity at the camp. Everyone thought that I was a spy. They could not imagine the kind of experiences that I had with time travel and genetic experiments. Craig told me that his mother was a radionic practitioner and wanted to talk to me, but I just did not want to get involved. More on that connection later.

The camp guard who processed the mail was a beautiful woman who I shall call Jane. An ex-marine with a body that could kill faster than a grenade, she befriended me and gave me my mail privately. Often, she sneaked up on me while I was exercising and made comments about my body. She was the cutest little creature that I had ever seen. I enjoyed our time together, but we both could have gotten into severe trouble if anyone knew. Jane allowed contraband to come into the camp for me and let me ship things out without permission. Eventually, she confided that my mail was the only mail she was supposed to read, but it scared her to death. She never elaborated on why she had to read my mail, but she said that she found me fascinating and the people who wrote to me very exotic.

At one point, I worked with an actor named Dack Rambo who was a star on the television show *Dallas*. Dack had contracted AIDS, and a Californian friend of my deprogrammer asked me to work on his case. Dack became a good friend as well as a client. He was controlled by his mother and sister who both made his life miserable. I was extremely upset when he died because the AIDS had gone into remission. When his doctors in Los Angeles insisted that he go for radiation and chemotherapy for Karposi syndrome, I warned him against it. These treatments weakened his heart until it finally stopped. I still see Dack in hyperspace, and he advises me from time to time. I promised him that I would fulfill his dream of opening a healing center for terminally ill patients. I hope to complete my promise to him some day.

My wife's boss was friendly with a congressman from Long Island. She spoke to this congressman about transferring me to a work cadre in Philadelphia. Using his specific instructions, I wrote a personal letter to him delineating my needs, what I wanted him to do, and added the facts that we had inadequate food, poor medical care, and the administration wasted government money on pet projects at the expense of the inmates. Imagine my shock and surprise when I found out that the congressman forwarded my letter to the warden! From that point on, I was carefully monitored and firmly admonished by the camp administrator. I had apparently embarrassed him in front of Congress. Fearing retribution, I promptly informed my wife of the situation. The congressman then called the warden who assured him of my safety. Within weeks, I was transferred to the military base in Philadelphia. It was adjacent to the shipyard where the *Eldridge* had been docked! I had come full circle.

My time in Philadelphia was brief — only four and one-half months. During that time, I learned that the government has vast stockpiles of materials hidden all over the country for use in national or global emergencies.

I was also told that under the base and shipyard was an immense array of complex tunnels and roads that were miles long.

I wondered if they connected to the series of subterranean tunnels used for high speed trains like the ones I saw and used at Montauk. These vehicles are so fast that they actually defy time and space. They enter into a subterranean hyperspace so that one can travel from Southern California to Maine in less than an hour! Our entire planet is crisscrossed with these tunnels and tubes. They were found earlier this century, and no one will admit that they know who built them. Aliens used them to travel back and forth to their underground bases. There are several entry points in the U.S., and the government has a map of all the locations. Montauk lies on one of the routes for these tubes.

I spent several hours on the phone each week with my deprogrammer. We worked with Richard Hoagland and NASA on a mysterious image being beamed from the "String of Pearls" comet that was approaching Jupiter. The image was said to be similar to the Jack of Spades seen in a deck of playing cards. Imagine my surprise when I heard this, for it was the exact same image that my grandmother had seen as a little girl in the mountains of Austria! As you remember from the first chapter, two of my grandmother's cousins fell dead to the ground when she directed them to look at it. Hoagland was interested in this story as well as my ability to understand ancient Hebrew glyphs and letters. Apparently, these letters were being transmitted to Earth from this so-called comet and no one understood what they meant. In addition, these letters were interspersed with hyperspace symbolism. The combinations of numbers and archetypes were confusing to NASA and other agencies who were studying them.

Every day, I called my deprogrammer and gave her the meanings of the latest set of transmissions. For the most part, they were instructions for the upgrading of human DNA and mind-patterns, but others were warnings about aliens and catastrophes on Earth. I understood these messages came from an advanced ET civilization similar to the Ohalu Council that communicated with me. The messages also stated that the String of Pearls comet was a created event designed to turn Jupiter into a sun which would in turn melt the nearby frozen moons of Jupiter and Saturn. This would then create many Earth-like planets that would be habitable for colonization. I was even given a listing of each unfrozen world with the possible population it could hold.

I was now down to the last six months of my sentence which I got to spend in a "wonderful halfway house in beautiful Bedford-Stuyvesant in Brooklyn, New York." Walking down the streets, I made sure that I did not confront any gangs. Continuous shooting spewed forth from a building adjacent to mine; we were even told to stay away from the windows at night.

During a routine sign-in after being out all day, I was taken into a bathroom by a security guard under the guise of being given a urine analysis for drugs. Once the door was closed, the guard took out Soviet satellite photos of Area 51 in Nevada and asked me to identify the buildings and runways. After that, he came to my room several times every week to talk about UFO's and what the government knew about them. One time, he became quite emotional and actually cried. The topic frightened him. He was glad that he had someone like me to talk to about it. After I left the halfway house to return home, he called and asked if he could bring a group of people to discuss UFO's, but he never came.

Shortly after that, my deprogrammer brought the author of "The Man Who Knew Too Much" to my home to interview me for a special HBO television show. Staying the entire weekend, he took my personal notes which he then kept for several months. Nothing ever came of the show, and my relationship with my deprogrammer deteriorated after that. She started taking credit for my information that I shared with her and told others that she had put it inside my mind when she visited me in prison. I soon started to realize how she was manipulating me and interfering in my fragile marriage. My calls to her became less frequent. Her calls to me were only to get information about the messages I was receiving or to criticize Preston and Duncan. In any event, I was glad to be home with my children and was trying to make my marriage work. It did not.

24

LIFE GOES ON

There were few jobs available on Long Island when I returned home. Finally, I accepted a low paying job in a day treatment center for mentally retarded and mentally handicapped adults. Because their auric fields and DNA patterns told me what was really wrong with them, I knew that most of them had been mistreated and misdiagnosed from an early age. This created additional stress for me since I was not allowed to comment on any client or their treatment. I longed to treat them with colors and mind-pattern alterations to improve their current conditions.

Working at this agency was worse than being in the prison system. People tattled on everything they saw. The supervisors were not much older than my children and had no experience in the real world. They wrote nasty reports on employees simply because they could. One had to be exceptionally careful about what was said or done in front of a client because anything could be construed as abuse. This experience reminded me of the Montauk days when the little boys were trained to work with the master psychics like Duncan. If only there were people watching those commandants to stop them from committing atrocities. Perhaps a higher power had placed me here to learn a lesson in humility and forgiveness.

These people were helpless and completely dependent upon others for their every need. There were times in my own life when I felt that way, too. I realized that to angels and ET's, human beings are retarded and developmentally disabled. Humans hope that higher beings will treat them with compassion and help them to advance. With this in mind, I made it my goal to do the same for the clients who were placed in my classroom. I opened a new seniors class for elderly and ill clients. Fortunately, none of my clients were violent, but many dangerous clients roamed the hallways. Although the staff was trained to deal with their outbursts, they were still injured on a daily basis.

The amount of money wasted by the state to care for these people amazed me. I suppose the state was avoiding another Willowbrook situation at all costs. Willowbrook, as you may recall, was a mental institution on Staten Island, New York that was exposed in the early 1970's by Geraldo Rivera. He went undercover as an employee with a hidden camera and filmed abuse of mentally retarded children and adults by state employees. This expose propelled Geraldo to fame and fortune. By perpetrating and tolerating this abuse, the state created an unnatural environment staffed with unqualified people who squandered taxpayer dollars. Beneath the facade of a mental healthcare agency was a regular business owned and managed by a few individuals who cared only about money. The people at the top made extraordinary money. The hands-on workers earned barely enough to survive.

While working at this job, my personal life fell further apart. My wife refused to try and make the marriage work. She became increasingly hostile towards me. Even though she cooked and did laundry for herself and the children, she refused to do so for me. Through all of this, I continued to clean the house and help with meal preparations.

In retrospect, I realize that she enjoyed her freedom while I was away and had become very independent. But, she failed to realize that her independence was facilitated by her boss, a wealthy lawyer, who gave her extra money for herself and the children. He gave her money for a new car and even bought our house under the guise of saving it from bankruptcy. There were also private dinners and dates. Under the pretense of doing nice things for my family, he was really attempting to get me out of the house and win my children's affection by buying them gifts. His wife, a Joan Rivers/Barbra Streisand type, turned her head away from the obvious. Unwilling to give up her life-style and social status, she allowed her husband to philander wherever he wanted. When I tried to discuss this with her, she turned against me and tried to use my Montauk experiences to prove that I was unstable and insane. As with everyone, I am sure they both will ultimately face difficult lessons that will force them to take long, hard looks at themselves.

During this time, I moved into a converted garage apartment on the side of our house. I refused to leave the premises permanently until the divorce agreement was signed. That way, my wife could not accuse me of abandonment. Because I had always been fascinated by the devices used to program me, and the ones that Preston had introduced to me, I used this opportunity to study radionics and eventually became a radionics teacher and consultant. My teacher was my friend Craig's mother, the friendly reverend in Florida. Caroline trained me via telephone, videos, and audio tapes. Together, we developed templates incorporating both dolphin frequency and ancient Hebrew archetypes to heal mind-patterns on the radionic machines. They are the only ones in existence on this world. For those unfamiliar with radionic templates, they are schematic designs used to form a basis for creating a new concept. In radionics, they are used as the source of a vibrational broadcast that is delivered to a target for the purpose of healing and/or changing a mind-pattern.

These circumstances also allowed me to continue the healing experiments that I began in prison. Photographing each client from my workplace, I took it upon myself to use these photos in radionic treatments for them. The results were impressive. Using my machines, I was able to keep the entire building under control so that no one got hurt. After I learned to recognize the electrical storm that builds in the minds of epileptics, I developed a series of radionic templates to stop the seizures. I also invented a hat/helmet for epileptics that removes the excess currents in their brains and thus prevents seizures.

I was able to see the strange auric patterns that exist around mental patients and learn how to change their auric patterns to a more proper pattern. This successfully eliminated aggressive behavior on many occasions. Actually, I learned this technique from the Montauk Project experiments. One of the experiments involved the psychic mentally altering a target's auric field to determine if the mind-pattern changed. They were trying to ascertain if the mind-pattern had to first be changed before the auric field could be altered. This experiment showed that changing an auric field was like helping a symptom. Changing a mind-pattern was going right to the source of a problem. Results showed that manipulating the colors and symbols in an auric field temporarily changed the mind-pattern long enough to enter the desired programming. However, a more permanent change occurred when the mind-pattern was changed first. This then affected the auric field.

One day, Caroline called to tell me about a woman that she had just met over the phone. She thought that this woman had a lot in common with me and that we would be like brother and sister. This woman was married and lived in Oregon, on the Idaho border. She was 3000 miles away from me. What in the world would I say to her and why? But, because Caroline had been so good to me, I could not refuse her suggestions. So, one evening I called and luckily got her answering machine. Leaving a hurried, matter-of-fact message for Janet Dian, I silently prayed that this would be the end of that. I called Caroline, told her that I left a message for Janet, but felt I would probably never hear from her.

In the meantime, I met a professional model at a class that I taught in New Jersey. When this woman walked in, the entire room lit up. Even though Mia and Jaime had driven down from Massachusetts to see me lecture, my attention was torn between them and this beautiful model.

25

JANET

After a few dates with the model, I realized that she would not be a good stepmother for my children. Still, I pursued her for her beauty. At the same time, I was also trying to maintain contact with Mia and Jaime. Much was going on in my mind. This included frustration and depression over losing my family. Then, while lying in bed one evening, the phone rang.

Janet's voice sounded so gentle and soft, almost like a whisper. Her angelic-like quality showed no trace of anger or hostility, all the things that I was accustomed to in a woman. Extremely shy during the first part of our conversation, she told me that she had never travelled to New York and had been married to the same man for twenty-two years. After exchanging background information, we discussed our current situations. The facts were that we were both married to other people and lived 3000 miles apart. In my mind, I kept thinking that I certainly did not need another phone pal.

The conversation turned towards my involvement in the Montauk Project. She had barely heard of it before but promised to get the books and read more about it. As I spoke to her about my Montauk experiences, I started to remember certain things about Janet that I did not consciously know before. I recalled being with her in a different place and time on another planet a millennia ago. Trying to push these images from my mind, new images flowed in. I saw her leaving her husband, moving East, marrying me, and having my child. For some unknown reason, I blurted all of this out in what seemed like a few seconds. There was silence on the other end of the phone for what seemed like forever. I thought that I had opened my big mouth again and ruined what could have been a nice friendship. Incredibly enough, she was receptive to these plans. We discussed the prospect of her visiting New York right after she returned from her trip to Peru.

When I hung up the phone, I realized that I was really out of line. Here was a woman I had never spoken to before. I told her to leave her husband and life, give up her lucrative job, move across the country to marry me, and have my child! I think I moved just a little too fast. After all, we had not even had our first date yet!

I surmised that after thinking about my call, she would determine I was crazy and never call me again. Surprisingly, she wrote letters to me and shared her memories of our past together. She also sent me healing products to calm my nerves and purify my body. When she called me from her office in Idaho, I always knew it was her. Sometimes, when I got the urge to call her, she answered the phone by saying, "Hello, Stewart." At night, I flew into hyperspace to be with her soul energy. We made love every night in this state and this bonded our mind-patterns in a special way. I thought about her every second. My parents and sister thought I was crazy to be in love with a married woman 3000 miles across the country. Remember, I was still living in a garage on the side of a house occupied by my wife and children. No one took me seriously. Once again, I doubted my own sanity.

On Mother's Day, about one month after I called Janet, my wife and I got into a terrible fight. She put the boys in the car, came back into the house, and struck me repeatedly on the head with her fists. The last thing I remember seeing was a chair flying at my head as I tried to stagger to the phone. After being unconscious for nearly two and one-half hours, I awoke on the floor of the den to see Emergency Medical Technicians trying to revive me. They took me by ambulance to the hospital emergency room where I was treated for a concussion and neck trauma. At this point, I realized that I could no longer keep my marriage alive. It was more dead than I wanted to admit, but I simply did not want to start over again with someone else. This was the fear that made me keep trying to keep it together. The truth is that I should never have married this woman in the first place.

Shortly after this incident, my final divorce papers were signed and I moved into my parents' home. The night before I left, I had another strange experience. Waking up paralyzed in the middle of the night, I saw a swirling dark energy in my room. Then I blacked out. When I woke up the next morning, I was so sick with nausea and stomach pains that I could hardly function. But, my best friend, Peter, came through for me as usual. He drove nearly 100 miles to my house, helped me pack, and took everything to my parents' home. I could not have done it without him.

That night in my new bedroom, I felt the loneliest and saddest of my entire life. I missed my children and my life with them. In prison, I lived on the knowledge that someday I would be free and have a life back with my family. Now, I knew that there was no hope of this and I would never be a family with them again. My heart felt so heavy. I was helpless and lost. I cried the entire night until I thought that there could not possibly be any tears left.

I wanted to talk to Janet, but she was in Peru and had her own problems with her husband. After she told him about me and her plans to leave him, he begged her not to go. Then, he called all of her family and friends to tell them that Janet was physically and emotionally unstable and should be committed. He failed to tell them how he used to beat her and threaten her life.

Janet was afraid that he would not let her leave. He moved into their guest house and took all of his guns with him. Janet's mother came to Oregon from Missouri to act as a balancing force to protect her. Janet left Oregon with as many of her belongings as she could quickly pack. Her mother shipped many of them to Missouri. Janet told her husband that she would return after her trip to Peru and work things out; otherwise, she knew that he would prevent her from leaving. Her intentions, however, were to go from Peru to Missouri and then permanently to New York where she would live with me. This was a tremendous leap of faith for her, but she was driven by an inner knowing of her future, as well as the desire to be released from twenty-two years of physical and emotional abuse.

During the time that we corresponded by letter, we both had similar memories of a distant past on a far away world. I was a diplomat and scientist; Janet was a teacher. Although humanoid, we were not completely human-looking. We were a couple but not married as known in Earth terms. Our home world was dark and grey with a cool temperature, all caused by an abundance of clouds. Later, we realized that this was due to the result of a massive attack by aggressive and negative aliens.

During a lull in the battle, I decided to leave the planet to find help and supplies to aid in the war. I intended to return before the next attack and make an offering to the invaders via a neutral third party. Because she was afraid that the ship would be attacked in space, Janet was totally against the trip and refused to accompany me. We remembered saying good-bye to each other at a launching point. It was dark and heavy outside. After touching her hand, I went into the ship with several other people. Here, our memories split. She remembers watching the ship launch before exploding and killing all on board. I remember a flash of orange-yellow light underneath my feet and outside the window. After that, everything went black.

I believe that incident began our physical separation in this universe. It took many millennia to reverse, and we had to go through vast periods of learning to find our way back to each other. I believe this experience is the root of Janet's fear of abandonment and my fear of exploding aircraft. Additionally, we both fear that the other will leave for one reason or another.

The day that Janet arrived, I went to work as usual but I was nervous and could hardly concentrate on anything. We had already decided that if we did not like each other, there would be no strings attached. I, however, was driven by a force that I could neither control nor explain. A few days earlier, I mysteriously found my only remaining credit card. It was to a large store. Once there, I used all of my credit to purchase an engagement ring. I also made reservations at a local hotel so that we could spend some time together before meeting my parents.

After work, I purchased a bouquet of wildflowers to bring to the airport. I then went home to pack and nervously headed for the airport. When I arrived, the flight was only a few minutes away from landing. Perspiration poured out of me and my hands began to shake. As I walked to the arrival gate with the flowers in my hand, a few stewardesses made comments about them as they passed by. I felt like everyone was looking at me. My throat closed up, and my boots felt like iron weights. Propping myself up against a wall, I was sweating, shaking, and dehydrating. I thought of bolting for the exit. What if she was ugly? What if she was nuts?

The plane taxied for the gate and passed a nearby window. If I left now, she would never be able to find me. As my chest pounded, I was sure that I was having a heart attack. The gate door opened to let the passengers through. They all looked strange. Maybe one of them was her and I missed her. What if she thought I was ugly or nuts and wanted to leave or refused to identify herself? I would be crushed. Finally, a thin, pale, reddish-haired woman walked through the door carrying heavy bags. It was the face on the back of her books* that she had sent me.

She looked very pretty and wore a white, angelic outfit. Before I knew it, my feet shuffled over to her and I handed her the flowers. As she took them, I realized that I had held them so tightly that I no longer had any sensation in my hand. As we embraced and kissed, she literally melted into my arms. She then sat down to collect herself. I was speechless and felt stupid. Nothing I said seemed to come out right. Janet seemed taller than her pictures and very delicate. By the time we retrieved the rest of her luggage and reached my car, I felt much more at ease. In fact, I felt as if I had known her all my life. She felt the same. Of course, on some level, we had always been in mental and spiritual contact since we had last seen each other aeons ago.

We spent a wonderful weekend at the hotel. When we finally went to meet my family, everyone got along very well. Even my children liked her right away. However, my mother explained that she could not understand how we

---

* Janet Dian is the author of the "In Search of Yourself" series, a set of three books that are a guide to knowing yourself through the Oversoul.

could be so close as we had never met before. Further, out of respect for my children, Janet could not live in her house with me so soon after my separation. My divorce was not yet final. Although disappointed, we had to work with the circumstances. Janet decided to return to her mother's home in Missouri until we could be together permanently.

Back in the hotel, while talking about my Montauk experiences, Janet used her abilities to remove an etheric object from my solar plexus. My whole being felt uplifted as this object came out. I did not even know that it was there. Janet explained that the object belonged to the lady deprogrammer in Massachusetts. With its removal, the woman would lose her hold on me. From that moment on, the deprogrammer never called me again! This woman then began a negative campaign against me and told others that I used her materials and distorted her teachings. If this was true, why did she ask for my help and advice right up to the day that Janet arrived? I believe she realized that Janet would now allow me to see the truth clearly for the first time and that she could no longer control me. Whatever the reason, she was now gone from my life for good.

The day that Janet left for Missouri, I cried until I had no more tears left. Hardly able to get out of bed, I was distraught because I did not know when I would see her again. I spent the next two weeks talking to her on the phone and sending love letters. Her mother was upset about our relationship but trying to cope with it. Early one morning, Janet called to tell me that the pregnancy test she just took indicated that we were about to be parents. With this news, her mother could no longer understand or tolerate Janet's chosen path. It was necessary that she return to New York whether anyone agreed to it or not.

Of all places, my parents were vacationing at Montauk Point. I had to tell them when they got home because Janet was arriving the next day. I nervously called a family meeting in the dining room the second that they pulled into the driveway. Everyone was tired and hungry. My sister had a sheepish grin on her face. I had already asked her to tell them about Janet's arrival, but she refused and said that it was not her place.

I began by thanking them for their hospitality and for taking me in after my divorce. Taking a deep breath, I continued by saying that Janet's mother was no longer happy with her visit in Missouri and Janet had to leave. Because she had no place to go, she was coming here tomorrow. She would only bring her suitcase; the rest of her belongings would be shipped later. Janet expected her divorce to be finalized within two to three months. Her settlement would allow us to move out on our own; thus, we expected her stay to be very temporary.

My mother and father listened silently to my speech. When I finished, my mother calmly looked at me and said, "Oh, is Janet pregnant?" My jaw almost hit the ground. Incredulously, I asked how she knew. She replied that my sister told them over a week before! How could she possibly have known when I only found out about it the day before? My sister then confessed that she receives telepathic messages from our passed-over relatives. That is also how she is able to make a Ouija board move quickly and give valid information.

At that moment, I breathed a deep sigh of relief. As usual, my parents were polite and kind. Janet could stay as long as she needed provided that when my children came for visits, we sleep in separate rooms in order not to offend or confuse them so quickly after the divorce. Although I did not like the request at the time, I do understand it now. For my parents to even allow such an arrangement in the first place was a magnanimous gesture.

Immediately, I called Janet to tell her that everything was okay. I missed her so much that it hurt. The weekend that we had spent together was so beautiful and perfect that it will remain in my memory forever. I had never before known such complete and unconditional love. A part of me could not believe that it was real. She was so peaceful and kind and never used a harsh word. There was never any upset or anger. I kept waiting for something bad to happen, but it never did. I found it difficult to believe that someone loved me so much and really meant it. After all of the years of abuse, manipulation, mind games, and restrictions, I felt like I was waking up from a long coma!

26

PARADISE FOUND

The couple of months that we expected to live in my parents' home turned into almost a year. Janet's ex-husband was difficult and refused to give her what was rightfully hers. Finally, she accepted a low settlement to put an end to that part of her life.

The pregnancy was not easy. At six months, Janet went into preterm labor. Frequent hospital visits eventually led to ten weeks of bed rest. My mother and sister treated her royally. I have been blessed with a wonderful family who always support me; even when they think I am crazy or hasty.

Originally, Janet wanted the baby delivered by a holistic midwife and was totally against the use of any drugs. However, her induced labor was exceptionally painful. In the end, she was grateful for the traditional gynecologist as well as the copious amount of drugs used to help make her comfortable during and after the delivery of the baby.

Janet was not dilating, and the fetal monitor started showing signs of distress. When Zachary was finally born by Caesarean-section at 6:05 A.M. (weighing interestingly 6 pounds, 5 ounces), the umbilical cord was wrapped twice around his neck. Without a Caesarean, Zachary would have strangled on the cord. Our doctor, an excellent woman, was both considerate and patient.

Within hours of birth, Zachary had successfully nursed and held his head up. He was not supposed to do that yet, but he immediately began to show signs of being an old soul who was not planning on being a baby too long. From the beginning, he acted as an adult. He drank water out of a regular glass when he was only three months old, walked at seven and one-half months, and said his first word at eight months.

For Janet, Zachary is a gift that she never expected. She is an excellent mother naturally. Even after many sleepless nights, she never loses her temper or patience with the baby. I admire her tenacity, calmness, energy, and devotion. She should be a role model for all mothers everywhere. I still do not understand how come she loves me so much.

Now that we have our own place and life has calmed down, Janet and I often talk about my memories and experiences. She is a good sounding board because she does not take everything literally, asks a lot of questions, and expresses doubt when necessary. Janet has enabled me to clarify my memories and explain circumstances that might otherwise have remained forever in a cloudy haze.

Because Janet is my "other-half," she is able to feel what I feel and able to say words that open up hidden memory segments within me. There is a lot of misunderstanding about the terms "other-half" and "twin soul." A twin soul is a separate entity that originated from the same spark of an Oversoul.* The spark split, becoming an identical, but separate, entity. Usually, twin souls do not

---

* An Oversoul is the "Father/Mother" of its children. Each Oversoul is the master identity that oversees its many subdivisions in many realities. Together, all Oversouls create the Christ Consciousness.

incarnate at the same time unless there are unusual circum-stances. An "other-half " is exactly that: the reciprocal energy of the same entity. These always incarnate together since their experiences need to be similar. "Other-halves" have one mind and almost one personality. They usually must marry each other. One represents the right-brain (male) and the other the left-brain (female) of the same personality of an Oversoul.

A twin soul is similar to two shoots growing from one seed. An "other-half" happens when one of these shoots splits and grows side-by-side. The plant world holds many analogies for existence. That is why the Bible refers to a "Tree of Life," and Jesus is referred to as the grapevine.

I sometimes find Janet's calmness and peacefulness almost unnerving because I am so unused to that. I find that I have to retrain myself not to expect bad things. Janet has taught me that I deserve all the gifts in the universe and that God provides me with everything that I will ever need. I always had that knowledge but have now learned how to put it into practice. Because of this, we live in a brand new town house, drive a brand new car, and my relationship with my children is superb. I also have a wonderful new job. I never thought any of this possible with my circum-stances. I can only compare my earlier experience to having a great new computer with every accessory except an outlet. Now, I have the outlet. It was always there; I just had to locate it.

I am devoting the rest of my life to helping others in any way possible. With my mental abilities, I give read-ings which usually include health counseling and mind-pattern analysis. I also help those who have had traumatic experiences of an unconventional nature and do not know how to help themselves. These people include survivors of the Montauk Project and projects like it, those who have gone through Kundalini activation, people who are possessed or who consider themselves walk-ins, abductees, contactees, AIDS and cancer patients, prisoners, victims of abuse or drugs, and people with mental illness.

I would like to take the knowledge that I acquired through my experiences and use it for the benefit of mankind. I welcome all readers to join me in an effort to save our planet and mankind from destruction. My life has taught me that nothing is impossible. The Montauk Project proved that whatever is inside the mind is possible to create. Let us all join together to create a perfect world where only harmony exists. Thank you for letting me share my story with you.

AFTERWARD

You have just read an incredible tale by a remarkable individual. While none of us are in a position to pass judgement on the objective truth of Stewart's personal experiences, we can safely make some conclusion based upon the obvious.

First, we can be grateful that our current times and moral climate do not necessitate labeling these experiences as the ranting of an insane individual. In years past, this information would have been dismissed simply because the prevailing mentality of the day would not have been comfortable with the implications.

We can also safely conclude that Stewart is a highly intelligent individual who fluently speaks over ten languages. Anyone who meets him personally will soon realize that he not only has the gifts of a high I.Q. and expanded intellect but that he is also blessed with an inordinate amount of ESP.

It is also evident from his life story that there have been numerous attempts to manipulate Stewart so as to access his rare gifts in order to serve various agendas.

The relative truth concerning the various anecdotes he has relayed are not as important as the fact that he has survived. In many ways, he is no less mystified as to you or I as to what exactly happened to him and how it fits in to what we call "objective reality."

The silver lining in his life is that the life force within him was able to persevere and reach out for the love that would deliver him from the clutches of manipulation. Above all, Stewart's life story is a dramatic rendition and deliverance of the highest aspect of love. The principle of love will ultimately be the salvation of each and every one of us. There is no other way. Thus, we had better start learning.

The most remarkable aspect of Stewart is his ability to interface with energies and phenomena which are typically described as paranormal or interdimensional. While these phenomena are not always easy to construe in human terms, Stewart views these matters in an organized, scientific format. He calls it the language of hyperspace. By this, he is referring to the symbols and archetypes within our subconscious upon which our words, thoughts and minds depend. While we all utilize the language of hyperspace on a continual basis, it is not readily available to our typical conscious mind. In our normal consciousness, we use only fragments of the original language of man. Sometimes called the "Language of Babylon" or "Vril," Stewart has a unique rendition of it to share with us. One of his personal goals is to give to mankind a workbook by which each of us can understand these many symbols which exist in our individual psyches and influence the daily life of each of us. When you begin to interact with your subconscious in such a manner, you begin to clear out the cobwebs of your existence and separate the dark from the light. Most important of all, the so-called gray areas become much less fuzzy. This is a language which will take us to the next octave.

I know this personally because in the process of working with Stewart, I have also become one of his students. I have experienced dramatic life changes, and I am only just beginning. In many cases, Stewart has exceeded the expectations of those who have sought his help.

Consequently, Stewart is writing a book, not only to teach mankind this language but to help each individual enhance or repair their own lives. The tentative title selected for his new work is *The Psychic Handbook.*

The information he has to share is so vast that Janet Swerdlow and I will be given the task of editing it in such a manner that it can be easily digested and used by the average individual. Although it will likely be more than one volume, our first task is to bring the flavor of Stewart's workshops and the intense practicality of his hands-on work into a book form where each one of you who reads it will be moved beyond your current horizons and propelled to new vistas of consciousness. Ultimately, this means happiness and harmony in your personal lives. Whether you are bored, abducted, or being strangled by a member of your domestic environment, there is a new reality which awaits you.

All of you probably know that I receive many letters and solicitations from people to help them with their various projects. Consequently, I have to pick and choose what I do very carefully. Stewart's future book is the most worthwhile activity I have found to pursue. I have enjoyed working with him immensely, and I look forward to what he will share with us in the future. Next, I would like you to hear from Stewart with regard to what he has to say on the language of hyperspace.

THE LANGUAGE OF HYPERSPACE

The road that led me to where I am today was long and difficult. I wish that there had been an easier way, but obviously it was my soul's intention to learn hard and unconventional lessons. My experiences left me with two major questions. First, what do I do with these experiences now? And, what benefit is served from experiencing all of these hardships?

I now know that my purpose is to reach out and help the people in this world, and perhaps beyond, to prevent and/or heal their traumatic life experiences. My goal is to eliminate the need for medical doctors, psychiatrists, and generally therapists of all types by teaching everyone how to heal themselves through analyzing their own mind-patterns. By determining where and why your thought processes began, you can learn to erase or undo the negative effects that attract your negative experiences.

This is not an easy process — only you can do this for yourself. If someone tries to impose a healing or correction upon you, and you do not correct the mind-pattern behind it, then the condition will eventually return. When that happens, it is sometimes worse than it was previously because you must be more motivated to initiate a final healing and correction. Negative impulses promote corrective action.

Now, my life's work is to motivate people into self-healing. I am creating a handbook for this purpose that will allow individuals to assist themselves whenever necessary. Included will be information on numeric values and symbols, how to receive and translate hyperspace sentences, dream analysis, mind-pattern analysis, auric fields, healing techniques, radionic templates, time travel, reading DNA, the Angelic Hierarchy, communicating with the departed, astral and hyperspace travel, and also a hyperspace dictionary. All these physical and mental healing techniques will focus on eliminating negative mind-patterns that prevent you from connecting and communicating with your true self.

The Mind of God does not think in low-grade standards like verbiage or written language. Instead, It thinks in color, tone, and archetype, creating the Triad of communication and understanding. Cosmic, interdimensional, and interuniversal, it is the basis of all creation. Those who understand the language of hyperspace can successfully communicate with any mind, anywhere, anytime. The language of hyperspace goes beyond space and time confinements. Understanding color therapy, which is part of the language of hyperspace, is a fundamental aspect of learning how to control your own mind-patterns.

Imagine falling asleep in your own bed or favorite chair, then suddenly finding yourself flying at incredible speeds over a strange land. The sky is a different color with multiple suns. As the scene progresses, you begin to see symbols that look like geometric shapes and weird hieroglyphics. Glowing in various colors, they arrange themselves in strange sequences. Information pulsates through your entire being, possibly agitating and confusing you. For a brief instant, you experience an all-pervading knowing. Everything makes sense; you feel absolute joy. Abruptly, you jolt awake with a light-headed sensation, instantly forgetting all the great information that you knew only moments ago. Your jaw, neck, back, and head feel tense — as if you have been through an extremely stressful situation.

Did you have a nightmare? Is it from the chili dog you ate for dinner? Are you losing your mind? The answer to all of these questions is "No." You experienced a trip to the hyperspace plane — where time or space do not exist and all events happen simultaneously.

This level of reality instantly demonstrates the thought patterns to your consciousness. Taking the form of colored geometric shapes, these thought patterns are called "archetypes." Archetypes are the visual representation of a person's mind-pattern. Whatever a person thinks, whatever ideas, emotions, or beliefs make up that individual, it is immediately shown in this colored archetypal form. The reason for the joy and the instant "knowing" is because you can now "read" for yourself who and what you are! You immediately forget that information upon returning to the physical plane because this information is not readily or easily available to your brain which is trained only to decipher the physical parts of life on Earth.

Underlying physical reality are layers of various energies that manipulate the atomic structures of all existence. These energies are controlled by MIND. To further explain, whatever is thought directs energies to create that thought. Humans do this automatically as individuals, families, racial groups, nationalities, and as mankind. Obviously, the larger the group which thinks in the same way, the more powerful and faster the manifestation on the Earth plane. This is how destinies of people and nations are played out.

The mind-pattern symbol of archetypes and associated colors is the most pure form of language and communication that exists, taking place on the God-frequency which is common to all beings everywhere. Using the language of hyperspace, one can understand and communicate with any creature, anywhere. As a consciousness descends away from this purity towards the density of physical realities, this pure form becomes tainted. The colors and archetypes translate through the brain as pictograms in the individual or group mind. Next, they become verbal language, then written language, and finally for very primitive societies, physical gesture.

Frequently, the dream state contains archetypes that cannot be communicated from the super or subconscious minds to the conscious mind primarily because the conscious mind is subject to societal rules which preclude attention to the unconventional. People who "see" symbols or visions are considered to be on the fringe of "normal." So, dream symbols are extremely important. Keeping a dated dream journal to review allows a message or important information to become apparent after you learn how to interpret these symbols. One of the reasons for the handbook I am writing is to help you interpret your dream symbols.

Mind-pattern archetypes have an important relationship to the physical body. Energies from the thoughts behind the archetypes create the DNA sequences that develop the body. Therefore, as you think, so you are! Mind-patterns create "sentences" of archetypes in groups of four. Four proteins comprise every person's DNA. Each protein is the translation of an archetype sequence into a DNA sequence. People who understand archetypes and their sequences can literally completely change themselves by manipulating the archetypes and sequences with thought/color. Certain color/archetype codes can unlock specific DNA codes. This will also be discussed in the handbook.

Guidance in this process is important to prevent uncontrolled Kundalini activation, or, the opening up of major DNA sequences before their appointed time. Without guidance, a person can become insane, possessed, terminally ill, suicidal, or addicted to chemical substances. Improper training presents a dangerous situation and is cosmically illegal. This might be compared to giving the keys to a fancy sports car to a child, then telling him or her to drive — it just should not be done! In physical reality, your body is your vehicle; your mind is the driver. Only a sane, trained, rational driver should be allowed to navigate your personal vehicle.

Anyone who has seen crop circles has seen archetypes. Most crop circles are complicated, comprised of several archetypes, or universal symbols, that must be dissected to be understood. Each crop circle is a sentence or sometimes even a paragraph. Who made them and what they mean will be discussed in my next book.

It is my intention that my forthcoming book will aid all readers in their quest to be discerning, careful, and knowing beings.

Stewart Swerdlow
is available for lectures, workshops, and counseling.
Services included are as follows:

- Color therapy
- Mind-pattern and DNA analysis
- Dream analysis
- Name analysis
- Alternative healing programs
- Special programs for mentally challenged; epileptics
- Personalized weight-loss programs
- Personal trainer for body, mind and soul
- Radionic programs

Those interested may write to
PO Box 1473
Lake Grove, New York 11755-1473
or call 516-447-0899
fax 516-447-6919
E-mail at expansions@aol.com
Web site: http://www.dreams-are-us.com

APPENDIX

For those who are not familiar with the Montauk Project and the previous books written on the subject, this prelude is designed to familiarize you with the story line of the entire series so that you may readily grasp the references to it in the present book.

The Montauk Project: Experiments in Time was released in June of 1992 and was a concise and summarized briefing on one of the most amazing and secretive research projects in recorded history. Colloquially known as the Montauk Project, the origins of this bizarre operation date back to 1943 when invisibility experiments were conducted aboard the *USS Eldridge*, a newly built destroyer escort. As the *Eldridge* was stationed at the Philadelphia Navy Yard, the events concerning the ship have commonly been referred to as the "Philadelphia Experiment." The objective of this experiment was to make the ship undetectable to radar and while that was achieved, there was a totally unexpected and drastic side effect. The ship became invisible to the naked eye and was removed from time and space as we know it.

Although this experiment was a remarkable technological breakthrough, it was a catastrophe to the people involved. Sailors had been transported out of this dimension and returned in a state of complete mental disorientation and horror. Some were even planted into the bulkheads of the ship itself. Those who survived were discharged as as "mentally unfit" or otherwise discredited.

Although the entire affair was covered up, research continued after the war under the tutelage of Dr. John von Neumann who had directed the technical aspects of the Philadelphia Experiment. His new orders were to find out what made the mind of man tick and why people could not be subjected to interdimensional phenomena without disaster. A massive human factor study was begun at Brookhaven National Laboratories on Long Island, New York. Brookhaven Labs got its start after World War II as the first major atomic research facility in the world. Prior to the war, the immediate area had served as the headquarters for the largest contingent of Nazis in the United States. They were known as the Bund.

John von Neumann was a logical choice to head up this new project at Brookhaven. Not only was he the inventor of the modern computer and a mathematical genius in his own right, he was able to draw on the enormous resources of the military industrial complex. These included the vast data base of Nazi psychological research acquired by the Allies after World War II. It was against this background that von Neumann attempted to couple computer technology with sophisticated radio equipment in an attempt to link people's minds with machines. Over time, his efforts were quite successful. After years of empirical experimentation, human thoughts could eventually be received by esoteric crystal radio receivers and relayed into a computer which could store the thoughts in terms of information bits. This thought pattern could in turn be displayed on a computer screen and printed out on a piece of paper. These principles were developed and the techniques were enhanced until a virtual mind reading machine was constructed. At the same time, technology was developed so that a psychic could think a thought which could be transmitted through a computer and potentially affect the mind of another human being. Ultimately, the Montauk Project obtained a superior understanding of how the mind functions and achieved the sinister potential for mind control. A full report was made to Congress who in turn ordered the project to be disbanded, at least in part for fear of having their own minds controlled.

Private concerns that helped to develop the project did not follow the dictate of Congress and sought out to seduce the military with the idea that this technology could be used in warfare to control enemy minds. A secret group with deep financial resources and some sort of military tie decided they would establish a new research facility at Camp Hero, a derelict Air Force Station at Montauk Point, New York. This locale was chosen because it housed a huge Sage radar antenna that emitted a frequency of approximately 400-425 Megahertz, coincidentally the same band used to enter the consciousness of the human mind. In the late '60s, the reactivation of Camp Hero began despite no funding from the military. By 1972, the Montauk Project was fully underway with massive mind control experimentation being undertaken upon humans, animals, and other forms of consciousness that were deemed to exist.

Over the years, the Montauk researchers perfected their mind control techniques and continued to delve further into the far reaches of human potential. By developing the psychic abilities of different personnel, it eventually got to the point where a psychic's thoughts could be amplified with hardware and illusions could be manifested both subjectively and objectively. This included the virtual creation of matter. All of this was unparalleled in the history of what we call "ordinary human experience" but the people who ran the Montauk Project were not about to stop. They would reach even further into the realm of the extraordinary. Once it was discovered that a psychic could manifest matter, it was observed that the manifestation could appear at different times, depending upon what the psychic was thinking. Thus, what would happen if a psychic thought of a book but thought of it appearing yesterday? It was this line of thinking and experimentation which led to the idea that one could bend time itself. After years of empirical research, time portals were opened with massive and outrageous experiments being conducted. The Montauk Project eventually came to a bizarre climax with a time vortex being opened back to 1943 and the original Philadelphia Experiment.

None of this information would have come to light except for Preston Nichols, an electronic genius who one day discovered that he was an unwitting victim of the experiments. Working for a Long Island defense contractor, Preston was researching telepathy in psychics and found that persistent radio waves were being transmitted which were blocking the people he was working with. A radio and electronics expert, Preston traced the radio signals directly to the Montauk Air Force Station and began exhaustive research that lasted over a decade. He acquired much of the equipment that was used during the Montauk Project and discovered to his dismay that many people from Montauk remembered him working there. It came to a culmination point when his cousin's husband insisted that he had been at Montauk. The two men almost came to blows over Preston's contention that he had never been at Montauk. Shortly after this argument, Preston began to get glimmers of a life he'd not previously been aware of. After talking to many different scientists and engineers who had some sort of association with the Montauk Project, Preston was able to put together what had happened. Somehow, he had survived on two separate time lines. On one, he worked at Montauk; on the other, he worked at a different location.

Preston's discoveries were confirmed when a strange man by the name of Duncan Cameron appeared at his door in 1985. Duncan had an uncanny aptitude for psychic research and claimed to have been trained in this field by the NSA (National Security Agency). Without mentioning his own ordeal with Montauk, Preston took Duncan out to Montauk and was surprised to discover that he knew the entire layout of the base and remembered working there. Duncan was considered to be the primary psychic used in the time travel experiments and also remembered having been aboard the *USS Eldridge* during the original Philadelphia Experiment with his brother Edward (now recognized as Al Bielek).

According to the accounts of both Preston and Duncan, the Montauk Project culminated on August 12, 1983. A full-blown time portal was fully functioning, but things were out of control and Duncan called together a group of people and decided to crash the project. While sitting in the Montauk Chair (a device connected to esoteric radio receivers studded with crystals that sent thoughts out of a giant transmitter), Duncan unleashed a giant beast from his subconscious which literally destroyed the project. The people who had been working on the base suddenly abandoned it. The air shafts and entrances to the major underground facility beneath the base were subsequently filled with cement. The full circumstances behind all of this remain a mystery to this day.

Although an unauthorized video was distributed regarding this story and several lectures had been given on the Montauk Project, no book was forthcoming on the subject. Different writers had attempted to undertake the task but were either mentally incapable of dealing with the subject or were frightened off one way or the other. One science reporter for the *New York Times* started the project but backed off when he discovered to his own surprise that the Montauk Project was indeed quite real.

I came upon Preston while researching an elaborate sound system he had invented and soon found myself listening to a spectacular story that was at least better science fiction than I had ever heard. After several months, I decided to undertake writing *The Montauk Project: Experiments in Time*. That book was written without consulting anyone other than Preston (who wanted to protect his sources). Rather than do a costly and time consuming investigation, my strategy was to get the information out as fast as possible and use the book to gather other clues that would corroborate or eventually prove the existence of this incredible story.

As *The Montauk Project* was published, further research and events continued that would indeed establish that there was a real scenario behind the wild information Preston was talking about. These were chronicled in our second book, *Montauk Revisited: Adventures in Synchronicity*, but the most spectacular of all these corroborations was the discovery that the Montauk Project was inextricably linked to the most infamous occultist of all time: Aleister Crowley, often described as "the wickedest man in the world." According to reports, Crowley had used the practice of sexual magick in order to manipulate time itself, communicate with disembodied entities, and to travel interdimensionally. It was even suggested that the the Philadelphia Experiment could have been the outward expression of Crowley's secret magical operations.

The startling proof of Crowley's association developed over a long period of time, but the discovery began to take shape in my very first conversation with Preston when he seemed to blurt out of the blue that he was connected to the magician Aleister Crowley. In an earlier life, he believed that both himself and Duncan had been Preston and Marcus Wilson, respectively. These brothers were twins and had been the first manufacturers of scientific instruments in Great Britain. In addition to being friends of Aleister Crowley's family, they had also been involved in a joint business enterprise with them.

All of the above sounded like one more wild story, so I began to look for any references to the Wilsons in Aleister Crowley's various books. None turned up. To my surprise though, I discovered that not only had Crowley visited Montauk (in 1918) but he had mentioned a "Duncan Cameron" in his autobiography. Subsequent to this, numerous instances of synchronicity between the Cameron and Crowley families were discovered, (these are detailed in *Montauk Revisited*), but I still could not find any references to the Wilson brothers.

The meaning of these various synchronicities (between the Cameron name and Crowley) began to be explained when I found out about a woman who called herself "Cameron." She is perhaps most famous for having been married to Jack Parsons, the world's first solid fuel rocket scientist and a disciple of Crowley. Together, they had participated in an interdimensional activity known as the Babalon Working (a ceremonial act which included sex magick and has been hailed by some as the greatest magical act of the century).

Through a further series of incredible synchronicities, I flew to Southern California on other business and met one of Cameron's friends quite by "accident." Soon discovering that she lived in West Hollywood, I suddenly found myself telling her in person about the Philadelphia

Experiment, the Montauk Project, and the Crowley/ Cameron relationship. To my surprise, she informed me that her real name was not Cameron at all. It was Wilson!

It now became obvious that Preston's story about being a Wilson could not be discounted nor could his general credibility be denied. Perhaps more importantly, it revealed that some very strange correspondences were at work that had to do with interdimensionality.

I would receive an astonishing letter several months later that would close the case as regards to whether or not the Wilson brothers had existed. It was from a man named Amado Crowley who claimed to be an illegitimate son of Aleister Crowley. Not only did he remember his father talking about the Wilson brothers, but he also provided clues which revealed that the odds of his lying about his parentage were nil.

Amado not only verified the existence of the Wilson brothers, he gave a spectacular account of his father's whereabouts on August 12, 1943 (the day of the Philadelphia Experiment). Aleister had directed a magical ceremony at Men-an-Tol in Cornwall, England where a large donut-style rock lays upright in the water. According to Amado, Aleister put him through the hole in the rock whereupon a line of rough water ran from the coast of England to Long Island, New York. In ancient times, a stone like Men-an-Tol was utilized in a ritual such as this in order to invoke the goddess. Obviously, a major occult correspondence was at work.

As *Montauk Revisited* went to press, another astonishing discovery was made. A photograph from the turn of the century turned up and revealed that ancient pyramids had once existed at Montauk Point. Further investigation revealed that Camp Hero, the name of the base where the Montauk Project took place, was located on sacred Native

American ground that rightfully belonged to the Montauks or Montaukets, the ancient ruling tribe of Long Island. Unfortunately for the Montauks, a New York State court had declared their tribe legally extinct in what some legal experts call the most flagrant case of injustice in the history of Native American relations. In a further instance of synchronicity, it was revealed that the family name of the Montauks' royal family is Pharoah.

The above information was included in the third book of the series, *Pyramids of Montauk*. Further connections were made evident between the Pharoahs of Montauk and the Pharaohs of Egypt. A deeper examination of Aleister Crowley's writings and the science of sacred geometry revealed Montauk Point to be an ancient grid point rivaling Stonehenge, the pyramids of Giza or the like. It was through Montauk that the project operators sought to control the evolutionary "computer program" of planet Earth in an attempt to influence how people and other life forms think, feel and develop. This "computer system" of evolution is identified as the morphogenetic grid, an ever changing and adapting program of birth, growth, death, and consequent recycling of the life force. It is this grid of evolution that certain mystery traditions seek to control. Many factions vie for the lead role in this quest to dominate. Evidence of clandestine operations at Montauk has since been demonstrated beyond that shadow of a doubt. Not only has there been testimony from personnel who participated in the project, but strange and sometimes illegal radio transmissions have been proven to emanate from Montauk Point. The local media on Long Island refuses to investigate the matter or even to seriously consider the proposition.

The release of *Pyramids of Montauk* brought forth world wide recognition of the plight of the Montauks. It was hoped by myself that public outrage would start the wheels in motion so that Montauk Point would be restored to its rightful owners. While some progress has been made, there is an unfortunate situation within the tribe itself. There are two rival factions which do not agree with each other and at this writing, there is no unified front. This has hampered the legality of the Montauks applying for legal recognition because the government is not going to recognize both parties. This is a very complicated scenario which I cannot become personally involved in as it is a tribal matter. The entire scene is further aggravated by political scandals and upheavals in Suffolk County and East Hampton, the county and town in which Montauk is located.

One of these scandals occurred when Robert Cooper, a Montauk tribal leader and East Hampton Town Councilman, was attacked in the press and sued for defamation of character. The lawsuit was from Tom Scott, the local police commissioner. Although Cooper had only requested that allegations against the police force at Montauk be "looked into," Scott ignited a huge legal battle which cost the town of East Hampton a fortune in legal bills. After a mammoth attack on Cooper, Scott finally dropped the case as he had no chance of winning it. The details of this case were covered in *The Montauk Pulse* newsletter.

Further evidence of scandalous behavior concerning Montauk was relayed to me by a court officer who had personal knowledge of the Cooper case. This person reported that during the legal battle, a state judge requested the District Attorney of Suffolk County, James Catterson, Jr., to conduct an official investigation to determine whether police abuse existed in in the East Hampton police force. The investigation was a whitewash, according to the court officer, with no police abuse being found. Of course, this turned out not to be the case. The police abuse was later proven and reported on in detail in the local press. Separate investigation of my own revealed some very interesting information on the official who "whitewashed" the investigation on behalf of the District Attorney. He is known for having previously stored business papers on the "derelict" Montauk Air Force Station. The irony was very bizarre.

District Attorney Catterson got into the act once again when he arrested John Ford, the founder and president of the Long Island UFO Network. John had visited me in March 1996 as he was planning to write a book that included considerable inside information on the Long Island defense industry and dubious political connections. A retired court officer (and not the same court officer who informed me of the above investigation), John Ford has a long standing reputation as a law-abiding individual who uses the court system to right injustices. He is also a meticulous researcher who covers all bases. In June, John was arrested for allegedly conspiring to kill three Suffolk County executives by sneaking radium into their toothpaste. The New York media and Long Island newspapers covered the arrest with gala coverage despite the ridiculous nature of the charge. It was even stated in some news reports that experts had determined that radium in such doses is not lethal and might take several years to have any effect, if any. Ford was also charged with possession of illegal weapons but this was dropped as there was no evidence.

The information on the alleged conspiracy of John Ford came from "inside information" that has yet to be substantiated in a court of law. The search warrant itself was dated after the search of John Ford's premises where cans of radium were found and seized. Those who know

Ford say he uses radium from time to time to calibrate his Geiger counter. Apparently, the entire arrest was a set-up by a "friend" who asked Ford to move some radium cans. The "friend," who just happens to work for the Navy, was also arrested as part of the conspiracy.

From June of 1996 to at least September of 1997, John Ford has languished in jail without a trial. A year since the arrest, there is no serious news coverage or any light seen at the end of the tunnel. Ford claims his own attorney is not working in his best interests. A prime example of this occurred when Ford's attorney arranged for a mental examination to be done on his client which declared him to be incompetent. This means that Ford will be declared a ward of the court and no trial will take place. He will probably be institutionalized. I mention his case to demonstrate the contentious behavior of the political climate around Montauk.

In the wake of all this, Long Island experienced the horrible tragedy of TWA Flight 800 where hundreds of individuals died as the result of an unexplained in-flight mishap. Although many theories have been put forward, the media refuses to seriously investigate the most probable cause of the situation: a particle beam emitted from a Brookhaven Labs facility which activated a nuclear missile. According to sources in the intelligence community, military exercises were being conducted off the coast of Long Island when a low flying missile was emitted from a flying craft. This heat-seeking missile was in fact a deactivated nuclear warhead being used for drill purposes only. As part of the drill, the deactivated missile was pursuing a heat-generating target tailing a C-130 plane. When the heat-generating target malfunctioned, the missile inadvertently sought out the closest heat generating source: TWA Flight 800. As it was designed to do, the missile circled the plane. At the same time, a particle beam emitted directly from either Brookhaven or a S.D.I. (Strategic Defense Inititative or "Star Wars") satellite, activated the bomb. The rest is history. Although the intelligence sources have officially requested that I identify the above theory as a "rumor," I do not doubt they are far off at all. The fact that the media has refused to even mention the possibility of a particle accelerator being involved is a sheer indicator that it was.

All of the above tells us that the political situation on Long Island is very hot. There is a trail of dead bodies from the crash and many of them are French. I have spoken to the French press about Flight 800 and they have interviewed Preston Nichols in more detail about the matter. I do not know what the French printed but people are slowly beginning to learn the truth.

The situation concerning Montauk itself is equally volatile. A political consultant who works for Bill Clinton told me that Montauk is the hottest political football in America. Between the mind control potential and the rights of the Native Montauks, this consultant said everyone is watching Montauk but no one is saying anything. As the electronic anomalies concerning mind control can be easily verified, members of Congress have no choice but to take whole matter very seriously. The Montauks' right to their sacred land is a straight forward case. Everyone in political control zones is on edge. This "edginess" can be viewed quite readily in the U.S. military, which took considerable heat for their alleged role in the downing of TWA Flight 800.

In early 1997, we saw a few close encounters between commercial airliners and military fighter planes. Intelligence sources inform me that these close calls were purposely provoked by the military so that their own air space would be more clearly defined. No one was injured but commercial pilots were made uneasy and forced to maneuver out of harm's way. The explosion of Flight 800 was apparently a result of a vague delineation of the military's right to access the air. If the particle beam was emitted on purpose, the military could have been set up. It is also possible that the nuclear transmission was some sort of accident. In any case, the military wants to distance itself from any more such incidents because they do not claim to be responsible for what happened. There is a mysterious variable at work in this entire equation which most likely comes from the C-130.

The above scenario betrays an entire breakdown in the power politics of the United States. It used to be, more or less, one united front that stood against Russia or the perceived enemy of the day. Today, we have unmarked black helicopters, U.N. peace keeping forces and upstart militias that threaten the sovereignty of the central government as we have previously known it. Many factions within the military, intelligence, and political communities are all vying for dominance. There are forces in American politics who want the Constitution to be trashed. The military, who derive their legally appointed power from the Constitution, do not want to be dismantled and replaced by a United Nations peace-keeping militia. The subject becomes rather complex and could warrant a book in its own right. The point here, and as was made in *The Montauk Project*, is that the powers behind the operation at Montauk were not operating within the legal laws of the United States or the martial laws of the military. They are a rogue group who infiltrate and use whatever institution or group they can get their hands on. In order to understand this group and the source of its power, we need to undercut the obvious, for if we stand up and rail against it, it can surely destroy us.

All of the above helped lead me to a further investigation of the esoteric powers behind Montauk. By tracing many of the previous leads, particularly the Nazi connection, I was led to astonishing revelations which demonstrated a trail of occult power that is undeniable in its presence influence. This has been revealed in *The Black Sun: Montauk's Nazi-Tibetan Connection*, a book which a new look at the history of the Nazis, the powers behind them and its esoteric connection to Montauk.

With Montauk, we are dealing with a story that never ends. It is the eternal quest to understand life.

GLOSSARY

chakras – Along the human spinal column, there are seven main nerve bundles, called ganglions, which are esoterically called *chakras*, a word which means "wheels" in Sanskrit. They form along the "S" curve of the spine which looks like a snake. For this reason, the chakra system is referred to as *Kundalini,* the Sanskrit word for snake.

DNA sequences – This refers to DNA sequences opening up in the body which is a form of Kundalini activation. DNA codes are the instructions that tell your body what to do and be. Some instructions are running at birth. These dictate that you will have blue eyes, two leg, two arms, etc. Others activate later in life, such as health conditions, abilities to play music, sing, etc. When the chakra centers along the spine open up, this is referred to as Kundalini activation.

hyperspace – A region of consciousness which exists outside of linear space and time.

Kundalini – A Sanskrit word meaning "snake". In esoteric studies and in the Hindu religion, *Kundalini* refers to the "S" curve along the spine which looks like a snake and houses the seven main nerve bundles, called ganglions. Each ganglion is esoterically referred to a *chakra*, which means "wheel" in Sanskrit. When people speak of "Kundalini," they are often referring to the "rising serpent," or when the "S" curve begins to awaken. This process is defined under the term "Kundalini activation."

Kundalini activation – This refers to the opening of all chakra centers along the spinal column. This results in activation of all DNA codes and sequences in the body. When activated prematurely, this can result in insanity, illness, and/or death. In most literature, Kundalini activation is associated with expanded awareness or heightened sensitivity. See also *chakra, DNA sequence,* and *Kundalini.*

mentalist – A mentalist is different than a psychic. A psychic merely observes the blueprints of reality and reports on them. This is known as a "psychic reading." A mentalist actually goes in and manipulates the blueprint in order to create a different manifestation. Machines and computers can easily read a blueprint for reality, but only a mind can change it.

Ohalu Council – A council of nine beings who live in a nonphysical world. Although they do not exist in physicality, they occupy the same physical location as Khoom, a planet in the star system of Sirius. They exist at a different vibratory resonance than do physical beings. The Ohalu Council govern the planet Khoom and the star system of Sirius.

Oversoul – An Oversoul is the "Father/Mother" of its children. Each Oversoul is the master identity that oversees its many subdivisions in many realities. Together all Oversouls create the Christ Consciousness.

radionics – A practice whereby a sensitive individual diagnoses and treats a patient through the use of an electronic device or template. There are many different types of radionic machines with varying degrees of success.

Wilhelm Reich procedures – These procedures involve increasing the orgone energy (life energy) in the body so that the mind can utilize it for psychic/hyperspace purposes. Some of this was detailed in the first two Montauk Project books. While undergoing these procedures, one is placed in an "orgone trance" where they are cognizant of their surroundings but are in an altered brain wave state which enables the individual to pull information he would not otherwise have easy access to.

twin soul – A separate entity that originated from the same spark of an Oversoul. The spark split, becoming an identical, but separate, entity. Usually, twin souls do not incarnate at the same time unless there are unusual circumstances. The term "twin soul" is often confused with an "other-half" which is exactly that: the reciprocal energy of the same entity. "Other-halves" have one mind and almost one personality. They usually must marry each other and always incarnate together since their experiences need to be similar. One represents the right-brain and the other the left-brain of the same personality of an Oversoul. A twin soul is similar to two shoots growing from one seed. An "other-half" happens when one of these shoots splits and grows side-by-side.

INDEX

G

galaxy   157
Galilee   73
ganglions   160
Gaza Strip   73
Geller, Uri   83, 174
genetic experiments   180
genetic manipulation   138, 156
Gengeeko   130, 131, 132, 133, 139
Georgia   64
German(s)   26, 27,
    67, 90, 161, 176
Germany   20, 22, 24, 73, 141
Gideon chaplain   173
Gideon's magazine   173
Giovanelli, John, Jr.   126
God   130, 146, 148, 174, 203
God-frequency   211
government   175, 176, 179, 182
(Stewart's) grandmother   182
(Stewart's) grandmother's
    cousin   76
Great Britain   155, 221
Great Lakes   175
Greece   62
Greek   78
greenish-grey creature   30
grey aliens   58, 70, 80, 84, 99,
    100, 101, 105-107,
    130, 135-136, 140, 141, 163
grey abductions   85
group mind   212
Gulf states   155
Gvar Am   73
Gypsy caravans   26

H

Haile Salassie   78
Haiti   135
halfway house   183
Hans, Dr.   140
Havana   133
Havana airport   134
Hawaii   154
HBO   184
The Healing of the Mind   179

healing   159, 160, 161, 163,
    188, 210
health conditions   160
health counseling   203
Hebrew   66, 67, 71, 75, 76,
    79, 109, 161
    ancient Hebrew   142
    ancient Hebrew
      archetypes   187
Hebrew alphabet   143
Hebrew glyphs   182
Hebrews   79, 84, 142
high blood pressure   174
Himalayas   30
Hitler   125
Hoagland, Richard   182
Hollywood   154
Hollywood producers   158
Holocaust victims   171
Holon   74, 75, 84
Holy Land   64, 78
Honolulu   154
hormones   58
hospital emergency room   193
human beings   186, 211
humans cloned   176
Huntington, West Virginia   167,
    170
Hyatt Regency Hotel   111
hybridization experiment   141
hyperspace   57, 81, 82, 86,
    88, 128, 142, 146, 162,
    181, 182, 192, 210,
    211, 212, 231
hyperspace academy   160
hyperspace experiences   28
hyperspace sentences   210
hyperspace subway   68, 71, 95
hyperspace symbolism   174, 182
hyperspace travel   210
hypnosis   168

I

Idaho   189, 192
illegal aliens   178
illegal radio transmissions   223
illness   160

238

243

THE BIGGEST SECRET EVER TOLD

*T*he Montauk Project: Experiments In Time chronicles the most amazing and secretive research project in recorded history. Starting with the "Philadelphia Experiment" of 1943, the Office of Naval research employed Albert Einstein's Unified Field Theory in an attempt to make the *USS Eldridge*, a destroyer escort, invisible to radar. The *Eldridge* not only became invisible on radar screens — it disappeared from time and space as we know it with full scale teleportation of the ship and crew. "The Philadelphia Experiment" was a total disaster to the crew members aboard the Eldridge. Psychological disorders, physical trauma and even deaths were reported as a result of the experiment.

Forty years of massive research continued culminating in even more bizarre experiments that took place at Montauk Point, New York that actually tapped the powers of creation and manipulated time itself. *The Montauk Project* is a first hand account by Preston Nichols, a technician who worked on the project. He has survived threats and attempts to brainwash his memory of what occurred. A fascinating account of the research, including the technological applications of changing time itself are given for the first time, along with Preston's intriguing personal story.

■ ■ ■ ■

160 pages, illustrations, photos and diagrams......$15.95

PYRAMIDS ᴼᶠ MONTAUK
EXPLORATIONS IN CONSCIOUSNESS

PRESTON B. NICHOLS
& PETER MOON

BOOK III
OF THE
MONTAUK
SERIES

THE ULTIMATE PROOF

*P*yramids of Montauk: Explorations In Consciousness unveils the mysteries of Montauk Point and its select location for pyramids and time travel experimentation. An astonishing sequel to the *Montauk Project* and *Montauk Revisited*, this chapter of the legend awakens the consciousness of humanity to its ancient history and origins through the discovery of pyramids at Montauk. Their placement on sacred Native American ground opens the door to an unprecedented investigation of the mystery schools of Earth and their connection to Egypt, Atlantis, Mars and the star Sirius.

Preston Nichols continues to fascinate with an update on covert operations at Montauk Point that includes the discovery of a nuclear particle accelerator on the Montauk Base and the development of new psychotronic weapons.

Pyramids of Montauk propels us far beyond the adventures of the first two books and stirs the quest for future reality and the end of time as we know it.

▲ ▲ ▲ ▲

256 pages, illustrations, photos and diagrams......$19.95

Journey to the stars–

with Preston Nichols & Peter Moon's

ENCOUNTER IN THE PLEIADES: AN INSIDE LOOK AT UFOS

*T*his is the incredible story of a man who found himself taken to the Pleiades where he was given a scientific education far beyond the horizons of anything taught in universities. For the first time, the personal history of Preston Nichols is revealed along with an avalanche of amazing information the world has not yet heard. A new look at Einstein and the history of physics gives unprecedented insight into the technology of flying saucers and their accompanying phenomena. Never before has the complex subject of UFOs been explained in such a simple language that will be appreciated by the scientist and understood by the layman.

Peter Moon adds further intrigue to the mix by divulging his part in a bizarre project which led him to Preston Nichols and the consequent release of this information. His account of the role of the Pleiades in ancient mythology sheds new light on the current predicament of Mankind and offers a path of hope for the future. The truth is revealed. The keys to the Pleiades are in hand and the gateway to the stars is open.   252 pages......$19.95

The Montauk Pulse™
A CHRONICLE OF TIME

A newsletter by the name of *The Montauk Pulse* went into print in the winter of 1993 to chronicle the events and discoveries regarding the ongoing investigation of the Montauk Project by Preston Nichols and Peter Moon. It has remained in print and been issued quarterly ever since. With a minimum of six pages and a distinct identity of its own, *The Pulse* will often comment on details and history that do not necessarily find their way into books.

Through 1995, The *Montauk Pulse* has included exciting new breakthroughs on the Montauk story as well as similarly related phenomena like the Philadelphia Experiment or other space-time projects. As of 1996, the scope of *The Pulse* will be expanded to embrace any new phenomena concerning the Nazis, Tibetans and any information regarding the various pursuits mentioned in *The Black Sun: Montauk's Nazi-Tibetan Connection*. Also included will be any new developments on the John Ford case and mysteries concerning Brookhaven Labs.

Subscribers are also offered discounts on most publications sold through Sky Books.

For a complimentary listing of
special interdimensional books and videos —
send a self-addressed, stamped #10 envelope to:
Sky Books, Box 769, Westbury, NY 11590-0104

SkyBooks   ORDER FORM

We wait for ALL checks to clear before shipping. This includes Priority Mail orders.
If you want to speed delivery time, please send a U.S. Money Order or use
MasterCard or Visa. Those orders will be shipped right away.
Complete this order form and send with payment or credit card information to:
Sky Books, Box 769, Westbury, New York 11590-0104

Name	
Address	
City	
State / Country	*Zip*
Daytime Phone (In case we have a question) ( )	

☐ *This is my first order* ☐ *I have ordered before* ☐ *This is a new address*

Method of Payment: ☐ *Visa* ☐ *MasterCard* ☐ *Money Order* ☐ *Check*

____ — ____ — ____

Expiration Date   *Signature*

Title	Qty	Price
The Montauk Project: Experiments In Time...................$15.95		
Montauk Revisited: Adventures In Synchronicity $19.95		
Pyramids of Montauk: Explorations in Consciousness......$19.95		
Encounter In The Pleiades: An Inside Look At UFOs $19.95		
The Black Sun: Montauk's Nazi-Tibetan Connection........$19.95		
Montauk: The Alien Connection................................$19.95		
The Montauk Pulse (1 year subscription)....................$12.00		
The Montauk Pulse back issues (the first newsletter was Winter '93 and is issued quarterly. List issues at bottom of page.) $3.00 each		
Subtotal		
For delivery in NY add 8.5% tax		
Shipping: see chart on the next page		
U.S. only: Priority Mail		
Total		

Thank you for your order. We appreciate your business.

SHIPPING INFORMATION

United States Shipping

Under $30.00 ....add $3.00
$30.01 — 60.00 ...add $4.00
$60.00 — $100.00 add $6.00
$100.01 and over ..add $8.00

Allow 30 days for delivery. For U.S. only: Priority Mail—add the following to the regular shipping charge: $3.00 for first item, $1.50 for each additional item.

Outside U.S. Shipping

Under $30.00.........add $8.00
$30.01 — 60.00...add $11.00
$60.00—$100.00 add $15.00
100.01 and over...add $20.00

These rates are for SURFACE SHIPPING ONLY. Do not add extra funds for air mail. Due to the vastly different costs for each country, we will not ship by air. Only Visa, Mastercard or checks drawn on a U.S. bank in U.S. funds will be accepted. (Eurochecks or Postal Money Orders can not be accepted.)